镜像

Mirror

[中] 易逐非 著
By Yi Zhufei

崑崙出版社・紐約
KunLun Press, New York

—當代漢語中堅詩人叢書—

特約編輯：　何中俊
責任編輯：　黑　豐
Contributing Editor:　He Zhongjun
Responsible Editor:　Hei Feng

Published by KunLun Press, New York
ISBN：　　978-1-949927-00-9　(Paperback)
　　　　　978-1-949927-01-6　(eBook)

Mirror
By Yi Zhufei
鏡　像
［中］易逐非　著

書名題字：　易逐非
出　版　人：　Victoria Zhang

出　　　版：　崑崙出版社・紐約
郵　　　箱：　Kunlunpress@gmail.com
發　　　行：　谷歌圖書（電子版）　亞馬遜（紙質版）
版　　　次：　2026 年 1 月　第 1 版　第 1 次印刷
定　　　價：　$40.00

Copyright © 2026 by Yi Zhufei, KunLun Press, New York
All Rights Reserved.
No part of this book may be reproduced in any form or by any electronic or mechanical means, including information storage and retrieval systems, without permission in writing from the publisher. The only exception is by a reviewer, who may quote short excerpts in review.

作品內容受國際知識產權公約保護，版權所有，侵權必究

作者介紹

　　易逐非,作家、詩人、文藝評論家。生於七十年代。筆名風塵布衣,號瞿上公子。詩觀:詩歌是詩人內心不斷生長的骨刺,有血的溫度骨代的質地。著有詩集《穿越滄桑》《瞿上人間》《且問風語》;詩歌、散文、文藝評論集《天堂倒影》;散文隨筆集《向陽而生》等作品。

About the Author

Yi Zhufe, Writer, Poet, and Literary Critic.

Born in the 1970s. His pen name is Fengchen Buyi, and his courtesy name is Qu Shang Gongzi.

Poetic View: Poetry is the constant growth of the poet's inner spurs, with the warmth of blood and the texture of bone.

He has published poetry collections such as Through the Vicissitudes of Life, Qu Shang in the Mortal World, and Ask the Wind's Whisper.

He has also written collections of poetry, prose, and literary criticism including The Reflection of Heaven, and an essay collection titled Living Towards the Sun.

序
詩意人生獨有的浪漫堅守

修竹卿安

其人：

生於七十年代的易逐非，筆名"風塵布衣"，號"瞿上公子"。以布衣之姿，懷詩心而立。他在文學與藝術的美妙歧途上，未敢稍有懈怠。數十載如日用筆書寫生命的軌跡，用詩凝煉人間的溫度，呈現文字的美、生活的真、情感的醇與思想的光。

其詩：

詩意棲居，是其一貫堅持的人生態度。從《穿越滄桑》到《天堂倒影》《瞿上人間》，再到《且問風語》《向陽而生》，每一部作品都是他人生的一次心靈遠行。

在《穿越滄桑》中，他用冷靜的筆觸書寫時間的打磨與生命的堅韌；《瞿上人間》則充滿哲思與溫情，那些詩句如同生活的回聲，映照出他對人世的悲憫與理解；《且問風語》則展現了他與自然、與內心的對話，棲居詩意，灑脫前行。

其詩歌氣象正大，取象不偏；境界深遠，著意不拗；聚力於句，用語鮮活；凝神於詩，雕琢無痕。歷時間烈焰的淬火與鍛鑄，愈顯難得的"金屬品質"。

其文：

其所著《天堂的倒影》一書，集詩歌、散文與文藝評論於一體，是其心靈的鏡像與精神的延展；散文、隨筆集《向陽而生》則像是他的生活哲學宣言；無論世界多喧囂，人心多浮躁，仍心向陽光，守住一份內在的清明與溫，這既是一種文學信仰，更是一種生命態度。

其書：

其書法蒼勁中帶著靈動，筆勢瀟灑而不失內斂。那種"骨中藏韻，墨裡有魂"的風格，正如他所說"書法如詩，貴在氣韻"。他以書法承載情感，讓文字在紙上再度呼吸。在他的世界裡，書法不是形式的美，而是精神的流動，是詩意在筆墨之間的再生。

其樂：

與音樂有不解之緣的他，致力歌詞創作。他創作的歌曲《包家巷七十七號》《人間煙火，東坡與我》《雲端的爾瑪》《編鐘王朝》《梨花的雪》《瞿上，時光的銘文》《黃河以西，史詩或牧歌》等，將文學的細膩與音樂的靈動融為一體。這些作品有的溫婉如江南細雨，有的蒼茫似西北風聲，每一首都承載著他對故鄉、愛情、時光的深情告白。他用旋律為詩注入生命，讓聽者在音樂中感受文字的柔光。

其心：

易逐非的作品，總是與"人"緊密相連——他寫鄉愁，也寫希望；寫孤獨，也寫溫暖。他不追求華麗的形式，而更注重情感的真實與思想的厚度。在這個快節奏的時代，他依然堅持以詩人的方式生活，不迎合、不浮躁，用一支筆抵抗喧囂，為世界留下一處安靜的角落。

其文字如水般清澈，又如風般自由。他以詩意為舟，穿越歲月的浪濤，不問名利，清淨致志。

半生文學文藝苦旅中的堅守，易逐非讓我們相信——在浮世喧囂中，仍有人以詩為信仰，以文字為家園；仍有人行走風塵，卻心懷天下的溫柔與浩然。

PREFACE

The Poetic Life: A Unique Commitment to Romance

Xiu Zhuqing An

About the Author:

Yi Zhufe, born in the 1970s, uses the pen name *Fengchen Buyi* and the courtesy name *Qu Shang Gongzi*. With the simplicity of a commoner, he stands with a poetic heart. He has never been slack in his pursuit of literature and art, treading the wondrous yet complex path of creation. For decades, he has written with a pen that traces the trajectory of life, using poetry to capture the warmth of the world, presenting the beauty of words, the truth of life, the richness of emotions, and the light of thought.

His Poetry:

Poetic dwelling has *always* been his steadfast attitude toward life. From *Through the Vicissitudes of Life* to *The Reflection of Heaven*, *Qu Shang in the Mortal World*, and then *Ask the Wind's Whisper* and *Living Towards the Sun*, each of his works represents a spiritual journey of his life.

In *Through the Vicissitudes of Life*, he writes with calm strokes about the tempering of time and the resilience of life. *Qu Shang in the Mortal World* is filled with philosophical reflections and warmth, with verses that echo life and reflect his compassion and understanding of the world. *Ask the Wind's Whisper* displays his dialogue with nature and his inner self, dwelling poetically and moving forward with grace.

His poetry is grand in its vision, choosing symbols that are not obscure; it reaches a deep realm without being contrived. The strength of his writing is focused in each line, and his language is vivid. His poems are finely crafted, almost seamlessly etched. Through the fiery forging of time, it reveals a rare "metallic quality."

His Prose:

His book *The Reflection of Heaven* is a collection that *combines* poetry, prose, and literary criticism, serving as a mirror of his soul and an extension of his spirit. His prose and essay collection *Living Towards the Sun* is like a declaration of his life philosophy. No matter how noisy the world may be or how restless human hearts become, he remains committed to the sunlight, preserving an inner clarity and warmth. This is not only a literary faith but also an attitude toward life.

His Calligraphy:

His calligraphy is vigorous yet lively, with strokes that are elegant without losing restraint. His style, described as "rhythm in the bones, soul in the ink," is, as he says, "calligraphy like poetry, valued for its charm and vitality." He conveys emotions through *calligraphy*, allowing the words to breathe once again on paper. In his world, calligraphy is not just an aesthetic form but a spiritual flow, a rebirth of poetry between ink and brush.

His Music:

Yi Zhufe has a deep connection with music, dedicating himself to songwriting. His compositions, such as *No. 77 Baojia Lane, The Smoke of the Mortal World, Dongpo and I, Clouds of Erma, The Bell Dynasty, Snow of Pear Flowers, Qu Shang, the Inscription of Time, West of the Yellow River, Epic or Pastoral*, integrate the delicacy of literature with the vitality of music. Some of these songs are gentle, like the light rain of Jiangnan, while others are vast, like the winds of the northwest. Each piece carries his heartfelt confession of nostalgia, love, and time. He breathes life into poetry with melodies, allowing listeners to feel the soft glow of words through music.

His Heart:

Yi Zhufe's works are always closely connected to "people"—he writes of homesickness and hope, of solitude and warmth. He does not pursue flamboyant forms but focuses on the authenticity of emotions and the depth of thought. In this fast-paced era, he persists in *living* as a poet, resisting the noise of the world with his pen and leaving a quiet corner for reflection.

His writing is as clear as water and as free as the wind. With poetry as his vessel, he navigates the waves of time, indifferent to fame and fortune, and remains serene in pursuit of his purpose.

Through his steadfast commitment on the literary and artistic journey, Yi Zhufe makes us believe that, amidst the bustling world, there are still those who regard poetry as faith and words as their home; there are still those who walk through the dust yet carry a gentleness and grandeur within.

目　录
Contents

序　詩意人生獨有的浪漫堅守　修竹卿安　I
PREFACE　*The Poetic Life: A Unique Commitment to Romance*
　　Xiu Zhuqing An　III

第一輯　梵音與般若
VOLUME I: *The Sound of Dharma and the Wisdom of Prajña*

梵音與般若　2
The Sound of Dharma and the Wisdom of Prajña 3

瞿上　時光的銘文　6
Qu Shang: The Inscription of Time 7

簫聲亂紅　10
The Xiao Sound Amidst the Red Blossoms 11

人間煙火　東坡與我　12
The Smoke of the Mortal World, Dongpo and I 13

大西北　牧歌與史詩　16
The Great Northwest: Pastoral Songs and Epics 17

光陰的裸顏　20
The Naked Face of Time 21

只此書香　24
Only This Fragrance of Books 25

落蝶之舞　28
The Dance of the Fallen Butterfly 29

藍花楹　飛鳥以及鄉愁　32
Blue Jacaranda, Birds, and Homesickness 33

命裡青花　36
The Blue Porcelain in Her Fate 37

梨花的雪 ──意寫金川梨花　40
The Snow of Pear Blossoms —Inspired by the Pear Blossoms of Jinchuan 41

心靈語境　46
Heart's Context 47

枯　萎　48
Withering 49

放　生　50
Releasing Life 51

一些預謀之外的情節 ──致下山的小和尚　54
Some Unforeseen Plots —To the Little Monk Descending the Mountain 55

歸　途　60
Return Journey 61

羽落鄉愁　64
Feathers Falling, Homesickness 65

山鷹訴說　68
The Mountain Eagle Speaks 69

隱喻的詞根　74
The Roots of Metaphor 75

母親的江山　78
Mother's Kingdom 79

先生　此別　84
Farewell, Sir　85

第二輯　突圍的另一種可能性
VOLUME II: *Another Possibility of Breaking Through*

所見 90
What is Seen 91

關於夏花的沉吟與獨白 94
On the Murmurs and Soliloquies of Summer Flowers 95

秋天適宜安放的調性 100
The Tone Suited for Autumn's Rest 101

天命辭──致自己 108
The Farewell to Destiny — A Letter to Myself 109

折春記 122
Folding Spring 123

有關驢的隱喻 128
Metaphor of the Donkey 129

突圍的另一種可能性 132
Another Possibility of Breaking Out 133

高處，鷹在言說 138
The Eagle Speaking from Above 139

風水與本命 150
Feng Shui and Destiny 151

柬埔寨，那些醒著或痛著的時光 156
Cambodia: Those Awake or in Painful Times 157

硯梅有香 170
Ink Plum Fragrance 171

五隻羊──兼致王小忠 174
Five Sheep — To Wang Xiaozhong 175

在冬天寫一些關於春天的詩句 178
Writing Some Spring Poems in Winter 179

落葉不哭 192
The Falling Leaves Do Not Cry 193

清明人間 198
The Clear Tomb of Humanity 199

狼　道 202
The Wolf's Way 203

最深刻的語言 206
The Deepest Language 207

油菜花 210
Canola Flowers 211

三疊人間 216
Three Layers of the Mortal World 217

瀘山祭 222
Lushan Rite 223

暗夜鏡像 226
Mirror of the Dark Night 227

有關花兒的預言 232
The Prophecy of the Flowers 233

驚蟄（外一首） 238
The Awakening of Insects (And Another Poem) 239

空　境 240
Empty Realm 241

包家巷　七十七號（組詩） 246
Baojia Alley, No. 77 (A Series of Poems) 247

第三輯　冥想的虛無及真實性
VOLUME III: *The Nihility and Reality of Meditation*

取珠（組詩）　254
Gathering Pearls (A Sequence of Poems) 255

泰安古鎮　258
Tai'an Ancient Town 259

暗夜如傷　264
The Dark Night, Like a Wound 265

廢墟上的寫意（組詩）　270
Impression on the Ruins (A Series of Poems) 271

編鐘王朝　276
The Zhou Dynasty Bell 277

被一張紙劃傷　280
Scratched by a Piece of Paper 281

俯仰之間的呈現　290
The Presentation Between Looking Up and Looking Down 291

恍　惚　296
Daze 297

節骨眼上的詩意　304
The Poetic Moment at the Crucial Point 305

敬畏白色　310
Reverence for White 311

靈魂的一次謝幕　316
A Curtain Call for the Soul 317

裸　傷　326
Bare Wounds 327

花語菩提 334
Flower Language and Bodhi 335

南有喬木 340
In the South, There Are Tall Trees 341

女皇 睡著的你還睜著眼嗎 ——寫在廣元皇澤寺 344
Empress, Are You Still Awake? —Written at Huangze Temple, Guangyuan 345

神話 陰謀與男兒美麗風骨（組詩） ——對話春秋男兒 350
Myths, Conspiracy, and the Beauty of Manhood — A Dialogue with the Men of Spring and Autumn 351

桃花，或生命意象 362
Peach Blossoms, or the Symbolism of Life 363

雨中靜坐 370
Sitting Still in the Rain 371

紙樣年華 380
The Paper-like Years 381

天堂裡 每顆星星都是鳴唱的蟋蟀 ——緬懷流沙河先生 388
In Heaven, Every Star is a Cricket Singing — In Memory of Mr. Liu Shaha 389

麗水金沙之柔軟時光 392
Soft Time of Lishui Golden Sands 393

邊緣隱居剳記（一組） 402
Edge Dweller's Journal (A Series) 403

金沙，再次鍍亮的不是光芒（組詩） 412
"Golden Sands, Not Radiance But Another Polished Truth" (A Series of Poems) 413

第一輯

梵音與般若

Volume I:

The Sound of Dharma and the Wisdom of Prajña

梵音與般若

一

夕陽　晃動蒼野的水聲
回到塵世最深的悲憫
從經卷裡起飛的神鳥
口銜妙法蓮華
從經卷裡走失的牛羊
再回不到青草世界

銅欽抵達迷途的岸
彌留般若的溫度
聖殿的長明燈河
泊滿往返天堂的舟船

星輝和麥芒抱緊眾生
誦經人穿越前世村莊
給掏心的人一點暗示吧
朝聖路上每一次匍匐
每一次長頭　可否抵消
一點兒活著的苦

The Sound of Dharma and the Wisdom of Prajña

I

The sunset stirs the water's voice in the vast wilderness,
Returning to the deepest sorrow of the mortal world,
A divine bird takes flight from the sacred scroll,
Its beak holds the Lotus Sutra.
The lost sheep and cattle wander,
No longer returning to the green world.

The bronze bell reaches the shore of lost paths,
The warmth of dying Prajña lingers,
The eternal light of the holy temple,
Boats filled with trips to and from Heaven.

Stars and wheat stalks embrace all beings,
Chanting pilgrims cross through past villages.
Give the heart-seekers a hint,
On the pilgrimage, each time we bow,
Each time we bow low, does it cancel out
The pain of living just a little?

二

天空和大地沉靜如昔
雪花和馬蹄盛開的草原
酥油燈　焰火的內心
受命的初雪如約
往返天堂的鳥兒
漾動輪回的漣漪

緋紅的大門緊閉
隱身的先知留下過往
被哈達和經幡注釋
民間由是安祥

白雲在仰望的高處閱讀
桑煙和梵音低回了流年
一切終將飲恨時間的虛無
酥油燈點亮的氈包
是生命最孤獨的偏旁
慢叩時光留白

II

The sky and earth remain as silent as before,
Snowflakes and horses' hooves bloom on the prairie,
The butter lamp burns with the inner fire,
The first snow arrives on time,
Birds come and go from Heaven,
Ripples stir the wheel of reincarnation.

The crimson gate is tightly shut,
The hidden prophet leaves behind the past,
Annotated with prayer scarves and scriptures,
The people are peaceful because of this.

White clouds read at the highest vantage,
Mulberry smoke and Dharma hum through the passing years,
Everything will eventually drink the emptiness of time,
The butter lamp lights up the felt tent,
It is the loneliest side of life,
Gently knocking on the blank pages of time.

瞿上　時光的銘文

一

兩江血脈
濯亮刀劍與犁鏵的抒情
蠶叢聚落
回蕩古蜀農耕的遺響
田園漫溯的暮鼓晨鐘
太陽神鳥和先祖
隱身未蔔的光陰

淩石橋的炊具　河池的石器
復活史前人類的銘文
友甯橋淌過三星堆文明的血
暗藏先祖遷徙的線索
三官堂藏種　金家院存珪
鏨刻先民衍息的圖騰
書寫黔黎煙火的神話

Qu Shang: The Inscription of Time

I

The bloodline of two rivers,
Polishing the swords and plows of lyricism,
The silkworm settlements,
Echoing the ancient echoes of Shu's farming,
The evening drums and morning bells of the countryside,
The Sun Bird and the ancestors,
The time before the dawn of light.

The cooking tools of Lingstone Bridge, the stone tools of Hechi,
Reviving the inscriptions of prehistoric humans,
The You Ning Bridge flows with the blood of Sanxingdui civilization,
Hidden clues of the ancestors' migrations,
The Three Officials Hall stores seeds, the Jin family's courtyard holds jade,
Carved totems of the ancestors' lineage,
Writing the myth of Qi people's daily life.

二

樹包橋　歲月的流蘇中
彈撥的風　來自遠古
吞吐日月的先人
用陶罐盛裝八百里江山
槐軒大寫天理良心
餵養精神的馬匹
生生不息

蜀都賦裡長出的稻花
華陽志裡升起的煙火
仰首　承天地清輝
俯身　拾煙火溫情
做柔軟時光的一顆水草
每一次搖曳　輕漾或顫慄
只為這水潤的幸福

II

Tree-wrapped bridge, in the tassels of time,
The wind plucked from ancient times,
The ancestors who swallowed the sun and moon,
Filling clay pots with eight hundred miles of mountains,
The locust tree's porch writes the way of heaven and conscience,
Feeding horses that nourish the spirit,
Endlessly.

The rice flowers sprouting from the Shu capital's poetic gift,
The fireworks rising in Huayang's chronicle,
Lifting my head to catch the clear brilliance of heaven and earth,
Bending down to gather the warmth of fireworks,
Becoming a water plant in soft time,
Swaying each time, gently rippling or trembling,
Only for the happiness that nourishes this water.

簫聲亂紅

花瓣　自簫孔飄出
是生命溫暖的胎記
穿行在我凝露的目光裡
該如何送別　這場逝水的趕赴

把自己打開或是徹底關閉
從骨殖裡捧一些清香的泥
種植這些餘溫未散的花瓣
種植一場秋意裡的愛戀
並以此　驅趕活著的倦意

從音樂裡拈出一條瘦巷
半角雨簷　紫傘輕攏
在苔痕漫染的心情裡
泊一灣江南煙雨
那宋代出走的女子
素手浣淨昨日霓裳

無須削髮　更不用落草
這一場亂紅　這涅槃後的光芒
將我收留於輪迴之外
　盡可憑弔　切不能喚醒

簫聲又起　我後世的愛人呵
你可記得吹響的
是我哪一根骨頭

The Xiao Sound Amidst the Red Blossoms

Petals drift from the flute's hole,
The warm birthmark of life,
Walking through my dewdrop gaze,
How should I say goodbye to this river of time?

To open myself, or completely close,
Holding fragrant earth from my bones,
Planting these petals still warm from love,
Planting a love affair in autumn's embrace,
And using this to chase away the weariness of life.

From music, I pluck a narrow alley,
A half angle of rain eaves, a purple umbrella gently closed,
In the moss-stained mood,
I dock a bay of misty rain from Jiangnan,
That woman who left the Song dynasty,
Washes away yesterday's neon robes with her delicate hands.

No need to shave my hair, nor retreat into the wilderness,
This chaotic red, this light after rebirth,
Will shelter me beyond reincarnation,
You may mourn, but never awaken me.

The Xiao sound rises again, oh my lover in the future,
Can you remember which bone of mine
Was blown through the wind?

人間煙火 東坡與我

一

三蘇祠裡　樓簷廊道
一花一木　一磚一瓦
流連的風雨都能吟詩
獨先生不語

憔悴千年光陰　銀杏不老
飽食千年月色　荷塘猶芳
獨詩文傳世的先生
魂銷骨立

升起在詞人筆下的嬋娟
憐見人間輾轉與飄零
化身燈盞　照亮迷途
照亮歸人不捨回眸的背影

進一步古赤壁
退一步短松崗
先生夢境溢出的浪潮
可否淘盡時光的沙
以靈魂的金　指引我們
安渡這危機四伏的年代

The Smoke of the Mortal World, Dongpo and I

I

In the Sishu Temple, beneath the eaves and corridors,
Each flower, each tree, each brick, each tile,
Even the lingering wind and rain can be turned into poetry,
Yet the master remains silent.

A thousand years of wear and tear, the ginkgo never grows old,
A thousand years of moonlight, the lotus pond still fragrant,
The master, who alone has passed down poetry and prose to the world,
His soul fades, but his bones stand tall.

Rising in the poet's brush, the graceful beauty,
Pity to see the world tumbling and scattered,
Transformed into a lantern, lighting the lost path,
Lighting the back of those who refuse to look back.

Step forward into the ancient Red Cliff,
Step back to the short pine mound,
The master's dreams spill over like waves,
Can they wash away the sands of time?
With the gold of the soul, guiding us,
Through this era fraught with danger,
May we find our safe passage.

二

鋪滿落葉的大地
是這塵世最溫暖的臉
空境如許　東坡與我
只隔一寸風雨

從峨冠博帶到一蓑煙雨
且聽那穿林的竹杖芒鞋
恍入隔世　借先生之風
化立身的骨

蟲聲如織的夜晚
適合仰望星空
不吟風骨不訴豪情
說沒了你的江湖
失魂兒的蕭瑟

今夜如昔　盛世的雪
爽約了北宋風月
准我靜沐先生遺風
從此　晴了餘生
滿盛這人間煙火
先生　能飲一杯無

II

The earth is covered with fallen leaves,
This is the warmest face of the mortal world,
In this empty realm, Dongpo and I,
Are separated by just an inch of wind and rain.

From the scholar's cap and robe to the rain-soaked cloak,
Listen to the bamboo staff and straw sandals rustling
through the forest,
As though stepping into another world,
borrowing the master's wind,
To shape the bones that stand firm in life.

The night is woven with the sound of insects,
Perfect for gazing at the stars,
Not speaking of strength or recounting grand passions,
But speaking of a world without your presence,
The desolate sadness of a lost soul.

Tonight, like all others, the snow of the prosperous age,
Misses the promise of Northern Song's fleeting beauty,
Let me quietly bathe in the master's lingering breeze,
From now on, clear skies for the rest of my life,
Filling it with the smoke and fire of this world.
Master, can you share one drink with me?

大西北　牧歌與史詩

一

青海湖掠出幽藍的夢
乍驚的水鳥忘情鳴唱
劃破戈壁漠野的寂色
格爾木　你懷抱的蒼涼
是那遺世的藥

曠古喜宴隱入民間塵煙
傳世盛典陷身時光流沙
火焰升起古老的圖騰
潮水撫慰疼痛的祈願

二

戈壁荒涼　大漠滄桑
誰的手埋葬前世的村莊
馱道和絲路丟失了驛站
耗盡紅塵憂傷

駝鈴幽咽　胡笳低訴
肋骨橫凸　野性的漠野
馬蹄和羊鞭一生都在
驅趕貧瘠和苦難

The Great Northwest: Pastoral Songs and Epics

I

Qinghai Lake casts out a dream of deep blue,
Startled waterfowl sing with abandon,
Cutting through the silent color of the Gobi Desert,
Golmud, in your embrace, the desolation,
Is the forgotten medicine of this world.

Ancient feasts fade into the dust of the people,
Legendary celebrations sink into the sands of time,
Flames rise, an ancient totem burns,
Tides soothe the painful prayers.

II

The Gobi is barren, the desert is weary,
Whose hands buried the villages of past lives?
The camel paths and the Silk Road have lost their stations,
Exhausting the sorrow of the mundane world.

The camel bells softly echo, the Hu flute murmurs,
Ribs protrude, the wildness of the desert,
Hooves of horses and the whip of sheep, a lifetime
Of driving away poverty and suffering.

三

從塵世迷途出發
戈壁讓時光陷入窮途
孤獨的鷹將孤獨的影子
插在大地上
刀子一樣

芨芨草覆蓋的漠野
把時光困守成留白
犛牛群用移動的脊背
接住太陽睫毛滾落的淚

四

三生石上的柴火　倒映
藏族少女手中旋轉的愛情
盛裝馬奶酒的碗裡　漾動
天堂乾淨的倒影以及
老阿媽隱忍的青春

靈魂遠嫁的人　可曾看見
大西北蒼涼的牧歌裡
一群藏羚羊　正在偷披
雲的衣裳

III

From the lost paths of the mortal world,
The Gobi traps time in its dead end,
The solitary eagle casts its shadow,
Piercing the earth,
Like a knife.

The desert covered in wild grass,
Imprisons time into a blank space,
A herd of yaks, with their moving backs,
Catching the tears that fall from the sun's eyelashes.

IV

The firewood on the Three Lives Stone reflects
The love spun by the hands of a Tibetan girl,
In the bowl filled with fermented mare's milk,
The reflection of a clean heaven ripples,
And the silent youth of the old woman.

The soul, far away in marriage, has it seen
In the pastoral song of the Great Northwest,
A herd of Tibetan antelopes,
Stealing the clouds' cloak

光陰的裸顏

把時間具象成箭矢
給牌坊的瘡孔以口實
把煙火抽象成饑腸
給古街的瘦骨以豢養
獨不能給牌坊下古街上
一根拐杖敲打的餘歲
任何詩意美化

從滿眼風水抽離線條
給碧瓦朱簷以蕩漾
從周遭脈息淬煉骨頭
給殘垣生苔以心跳
獨不能給天光下春色中
彎曲的脊柱和雙膝
接不住一粒塵埃的悽惶
任何浪漫修飾

風過簷角　瓦當輕響
把急景緩成半闋留白
這古鎮　一切過往及遭逢
躲不開白駒過隙揚塵的灰
朝聞故居的炊煙化了熱血
東嶽廟的香火還了昨天的債
大鴻米店打的是明天的烊

The Naked Face of Time

Shape time into arrows,
Give the pockmarks of the archway a voice,
Turn fireworks into hunger,
And nourish the ancient street's bony frame.
But cannot give the ancient street under the archway,
The remaining years to be struck by a cane—
No poetry can beautify that.

Extract the lines from the full view of Feng Shui,
Give the green tiles and red eaves a ripple,
Temper bones from the pulse of the surroundings,
Give the crumbling walls and moss a heartbeat.
But cannot give the bending spine and knees,
Under the daylight and spring's colors,
The helplessness of not catching a single speck of dust.
No romantic embellishments.

The wind passes the eaves, the tiles faintly chime,
Turn a swift scene into a half-moon of blank space.
This ancient town, all the past and encounters,
Cannot escape the dust of the white horse galloping through the gap.
In the morning, the smoke from the old house has turned to hot blood,
The incense at the Eastern Mountain Temple repays yesterday's debts,
The big rice shop prepares for tomorrow's closure.

麻窩草鞋織就一代人命運
油紙傘撐開一方水土晴空
老鷹茶裡的鷹拒絕落塵
趕黃草醒的是醉酒的魂
矗龍的淚滴落成井
嘗一口　不說甜心就會痛
如是　我們予生活以妄念
生活饋我們以幻象

此刻　蒼顏鶴髮的母親
拐杖敲打的光陰真實
大半生寫進骨髓裡
命運的冷光陰的鏽真實
佝僂的身子離地心引力
近得只差一次心跳
古鎮老街拐杖敲打的光陰
連回聲都是痛的

The straw shoes woven from hemp thread spin a generation's fate,
The oiled-paper umbrella opens a sky above the land,
The eagle in the tea refuses to fall into dust,
The yellow grass awakens the drunken soul,
Nie Long's tears drop into the well,
Taste a drop, and if you don't say sweet, the heart will ache.
Thus, we give life our delusions,
And life gifts us illusions in return.

At this moment, the mother with pale face and crane's hair,
The real passage of time struck by the cane,
A lifetime written into the marrow,
The cold glow of fate, the rust of time, all are real.
The hunched body nearly escapes the force of gravity,
A hair's breadth away from the next heartbeat.
The ancient street under the cane's strike,
Even the echoes are painful.

只此書香

一

故居老宅的九級臺階
硌疼時代森冷的意志
泥濘的田坎上　冬天
光著腳板出發的小少年
從山遠水遠的十萬大山
躬身接過生活沉重的命題
像接過宿命鉛封的神諭

二

樹葉捂滅理想的光芒
鳥翅搬弄別處的風月
孤獨的群山　孤獨的堰塘
孤獨木排上孤獨的小書生
嗆在葉子煙鍋裡的背影
像臨風的枯樹皮
耗盡最後的水滴

Only This Fragrance of Books

I

The nine steps of the old home's staircase,
Grinds against the cold, rigid will of an era,
On the muddy dike, in winter,
A young boy sets out barefoot.
From the distant mountains and rivers,
He bends to take on the heavy task of life,
Like receiving a divine prophecy sealed in lead by fate.

II

Leaves smother the light of ideals,
Bird wings stir the winds of distant affairs,
The lonely mountains, the lonely ponds,
On the solitary raft, a lonely scholar,
His shadow choked in the smoke of leaves,
Like the bark of a tree facing the wind,
Exhausting the last drop of water.

三

從巨大樹洞接過山頭
扛在肩上　從此一生
鹽的哲學覆蓋雪的隱喻
鷹的歎息從仰望的高處
落下　劃過脊背的流星
照見火苗之外
人世最深的荒

四

懷抱活命的溪流　火塘
攥緊山裡人生息的命脈
跌宕於宿命之外的思緒
是火狐劃過原野的孤獨
更是鄉愁飲恨時光的殤
如今　再不能帶你遠行
看人世春暖花開
看紅塵嫵媚
只此書香　嫋娜
從此　天上人間

III

From the vast tree hollow, he takes the mountaintop,
Carrying it on his shoulders for the rest of his life,
The philosophy of salt covers the metaphor of snow,
The eagle's sigh falls from its high vantage,
A meteor traces across his back,
Revealing the deepest desolation of the human world
Beyond the flames.

IV

Embracing the stream of life, the hearth,
Clutching the lifeblood of life in the mountains,
Tossed thoughts beyond fate,
Like a fox's lonely path across the fields,
More so, the homesickness, the sorrow of time.
Now, I can no longer take you far,
To witness the world's spring bloom,
To see the worldly charm.
Only this fragrance of books, gentle,
From now on, in the heavens and on earth.

落蝶之舞

深入靈魂的弓弦揉撚音符
讓這世界有了霧態的遼闊
我藏身一粒巨大的休止符
等待破繭

當下一次心跳註定成為懸念
杜普蕾　請以殤
賜我以腐爛的光芒

法蘭西　不知名的小村莊
時間　以魚的姿態滑過天荒
滑過一隻　落蝶的寂寞
什麼樣的結局　都是遺憾

把自己葬在一首詩歌
以及被你催眠的世界
以徹底的靜默對抗命運的未葡

在我看來　大提琴及以命相許的你
極柔是情深　至剛是決絕
音符間的滯留　是你不屑的平庸

上帝說　所有靈魂都是溫暖的
你卻在琴聲裡訴盡人世清醒的冷
忘記留一點餘溫　給塵世打烊

The Dance of the Fallen Butterfly

Deep within the soul's strings, I twist the notes,
To let this world have a fog-like vastness,
I hide within a massive rest,
Waiting for the cocoon to break.

When the next heartbeat is destined to become a suspense,
Du Pre, please, with sorrow,
Grant me the rotting light.

In France, in an unnamed village,
Time glides like a fish over endless skies,
It slips past the loneliness of a fallen butterfly,
No matter the ending, it is all regret.

I bury myself in a poem,
And in the world you hypnotize,
With utter silence, I fight fate's unfolding.

To me, the cello and you, whom I would give my life,
So tender in your affection, so resolute in your departure,
The pause between the notes is your disdain for the mundane.

God said, all souls are warm,
But you in your music, speak of the cold, awake truth of the world,
Forgetting to leave a little warmth behind,
To close the door of this earthly realm.

琴聲以遠　夏花成為苟且者的謊言
你用四十二年光陰　留下絕響
讓我們聽見白玫瑰失血的倔強

浪漫如法蘭西　容不下紫色的愛戀
不是每只貝殼都在星光裡打開心事
你遺世的殤其實是骨殖裡的香

當我懷抱音樂和詩歌的亡靈
在琴聲中睡去　請相信
世界的盡頭　亦溫暖如昔

The cello's sound fades, summer flowers become lies for the complacent,
You left the final sound after forty-two years,
Letting us hear the stubbornness of a white rose's bleeding.

Romantic as France, unable to hold the purple love,
Not every shell opens its heart in the starlight,
Your unspoken sorrow is, in fact, the fragrance within your bones.

When I embrace the ghosts of music and poetry,
Sleeping away in the sound of the cello, please believe,
The end of the world is still as warm as it ever was.

藍花楹　飛鳥以及鄉愁

一

院子裡的藍花楹
在一場嚴寒的霜凍裡
丟失了故鄉的記憶

瓦舍簷角的臂彎裡
青夢盛開藍色焰火
這深入風雨內心的鄉愁
像極了我走失的青春

閉了眼　總有一息星輝
三兩聲蟲鳴　落入杯中
激蕩命運深處的迴響

無根的空落
置我結局之外　橫刀方知
有一種致命叫藍花楹的藍
有一種涅槃叫藍花楹的毒

Blue Jacaranda, Birds, and Homesickness

I

The blue jacaranda in the courtyard,
Loses the memory of its hometown
In a severe frost.

In the curve of the eaves,
The green dream blooms blue fireworks,
This homesickness, deep within the wind and rain,
Resembling the youth I have lost.

When I close my eyes, a flicker of starlight remains,
The chirping of a few insects falls into my cup,
Stirring echoes deep in the depths of destiny.

Rootless emptiness,
Places me beyond the end,
Only when the sword is drawn do I realize,
There's a deadly blue called blue jacaranda,
And a rebirth, a poison, called the blue of jacaranda.

二

霓虹輕薄熟透的夜色
煙鬥暗示生存的迷局
誰的手　攥緊又鬆開

胎記一般
書寫宿命密碼的男人
在這如水星夜　趕赴
一枚野草握緊的彼岸

將我和塵世一同叫醒
自故鄉森林而來的鳥兒
熱切的俯衝撞破時空的冷

天空那麼近　人間那麼遠
飛翼與利喙之間
拾荒的人　在文字裡尋找
曾經呼嘯天際的羽毛

II

The thin, ripe night of neon,
The smoke from a pipe hints at life's maze,
Whose hand tightly grips and then releases?

Like a birthmark,
A man writing the fate's code,
In this watery Mercury night, rushing
To the other shore, tightly gripped by wild grass.

Awake me with the world,
The bird from the forest of my hometown,
Diving eagerly, shattering the cold of time and space.

The sky so near, the world so far,
Between wings and sharp beaks,
A scavenger in search of words,
Looking for the feathers that once howled across the sky.

命裡青花

一

她隨手畫下窗櫺和柵欄
吹一口氣　水色洇開
指尖輕彈　墨凝成土
在陽光繾綣裡　種花種草
種一些憂傷的瓷器
那些花兒　都是她的兵馬
與命運狹路相逢
而瓷器　是未來的自己
提前邂逅的結局

隱去的萬水千山
是候鳥溫暖的歸途
掠過的風暴雷霆
是花兒潔白的修行
在天為雲　落地成花
時間火焰鎖住的水墨
每一滴都是圓滿的輪回

The Blue Porcelain in Her Fate

I

She casually sketches the window bars and fence,
Breathing out, the watercolors spread,
Her fingertips lightly flick, the ink into earth,
In the warmth of sunlight, she plants flowers and grass,
Planting pieces of porcelain, tinged with sorrow.
Those flowers are her army,
Meeting destiny on a narrow road,
While the porcelain,
Is the future self,
Encountering its conclusion ahead of time.

The thousands of mountains and rivers that have been hidden,
Are the warm return of migratory birds,
The storms and thunder that have passed,
Are the flowers' pure practice.
In the sky as clouds,
On the ground as flowers,
Every drop of ink locked in the flame of time,
Is a perfect cycle of reincarnation.

二

是怎樣一次動念
賦予女人命犯青花的勇氣
又是怎樣一次碎裂
成就女人命定青花的絕唱
筆鋒流淌釉色
曠遠　如月華流動的水聲
清寂　似時光彌散的沉香
一張紙的潔白其實是女人
一生的潔白

一個女人的詩意
洞開無數人的遠方
一個女人的遠方
喚醒無數人的詩意
而我洗心革面的出發
不為拈花　也不為送香
只為觸摸命裡的青花

II

How did a single thought,
Give the woman the courage to face the blue porcelain fate?
And how did a single shattering,
Create the woman's definitive blue porcelain elegy?
The brush flows with glaze,
Vast, like the sound of water flowing under the moonlight,
Silent, like the incense fading in time,
The whiteness of a single sheet of paper is, in fact,
The purity of a woman's entire life.

A woman's poetry,
Opens countless distant places,
A woman's distant place,
Awakens countless poetry,
And I, setting off with a cleansed heart,
Not to pick flowers, nor to send fragrance,
But only to touch the blue porcelain in my fate.

梨花的雪
——意寫金川梨花

一

三月　天空藏起藍色的鏡子
秘境中　一場盛大的花事
翻越覆雪的金頂

二

埋藏金脈最後線索的土地
高聳的碉樓　並不執著
刻畫時光飲恨的孤獨
馬奈鍋莊的篝火中
疾馳的馬蹄　揚起
漫天　梨花的雪

三

人間有多沸騰
大金川河的內心就有多肅靜
端坐河流之上　群山若佛
打坐　誦經　拈花　拂塵
梨花打掃乾淨的時空
東女美人兒復活了傳奇

The Snow of Pear Blossoms
—*Inspired by the Pear Blossoms of Jinchuan*

I

In March, the sky hides its blue mirror,
In the secret realm, a grand floral affair unfolds,
Climbing over the snow-covered Golden Peak.

II

The land that buries the final clue of the gold vein,
The towering watchtowers are not persistent,
Carving the solitude of time's bitter drink,
In the bonfire of the Manai Pot,
The galloping hooves rise,
Sending pear blossom snow across the sky.

III

The more the world boils with fervor,
The quieter is the heart of the Dajinchuan River.
Sitting atop the river, the mountains like Buddhas,
Meditating, chanting, plucking flowers, dusting away the dirt,
The pear blossoms sweep the time and space clean,
The Eastern Beauty has resurrected the legend.

四

天地空境　最讓人動容的
不是時間之上金黃的結局
而是分蘖之前　枝頭
一意孤行的初念

五

鷹總是如期捎回天堂的訊息
總有老阿媽油燈撥亮的歸途
在梨花鋪滿的流年
寫下鄉愁　每一滴
都潔白如鹽

六

這個三月　無需桃紅櫻粉
也無需任何粉飾與頌詞
任這大淨之地　梨花的雪
驅逐幻想　剝去偽裝
一證人世清白

IV

In the empty realm of heaven and earth,
What touches the heart the most,
Is not the golden conclusion above time,
But the first thought,
Stubbornly blooming on the branch before the sprouting.

V

The eagle always brings back messages from heaven on time,
There's always the return path lit by an old woman's oil lamp,
In the years paved with pear blossoms,
Writing down homesickness,
Each drop, as pure as a silkworm.

VI

This March, no need for peach pink or cherry blossom powder,
No need for adornment or praise,
Let this land of purity, the snow of pear blossoms,
Drive away illusions, peel off disguises,
Proving the purity of the world.

七

從人間出發的梨花
與落草人間的月
誰是誰的前世今生
且等煙火餵養的風骨
帶梨花回到最初的枝頭
帶詩歌回到母語的故鄉

八

鷹翅抖落天堂的霜
祈願掉進塵埃的傷
余溫尤暖的天地之間
融化消弭抑或飛升涅槃
每一步　都是使命的召喚

九

叩訪秘境的詩人呵
你打馬經過　可曾邂逅
梨花雪中迷路的書生
終日吞咽塵世麥芒
斷了歸途　且舉杯
你敬詩歌
我敬故鄉

VII

The pear blossoms departing from the world,
And the moon falling into the world,
Who is whose past and present life?
Wait for the wind, nourished by fireworks,
To bring the pear blossoms back to the original branch,
To bring poetry back to the homeland of mother tongue.

VIII

The eagle's wings shake off the frost of heaven,
Praying for the wounds that fall into the dust,
In the warmth lingering between heaven and earth,
Melting, dissipating, or ascending to nirvana,
Every step is a summons of destiny.

IX

Poet, visiting the secret realm,
As you ride past, have you encountered
The scholar lost in the snow of pear blossoms?
Swallowing the world's dust and wheat bristles all day,
Cutting off the return path, yet raising a cup,
You toast to poetry,
And I toast to my hometown.

心靈語境

只是七枚音符之間
綻開的曼妙世界
甜蜜和痛楚此起彼伏
而我　用盡十萬詞匯
也寫不出一首貼心的好詩

這是多麼適宜心靈安放的調式
這是多麼適宜靈魂歸真的語境
如此　請別在視野裡種植冰菊
讓我悽惶於含苞待放的苦難

我相信　我未曾經歷的某段遭遇
就端坐在這樣一首曲子裡
也或許是兩枚音符之間
我即可飲盡生命的腐朽
亦能暢寫愛情的傳奇

自內心飛出的小鳥
終被這箏的纏綿弄哭
心河的波光潰決了表情的堤岸
這時候　無數詩歌意念盤旋
卻遲遲落不到
我靈魂的天葬台

Heart's Context

It is just between seven notes,
A delicate world unfurls.
Sweetness and pain rise and fall,
Yet I, with a hundred thousand words,
Can never write a poem close enough to the heart.

This is such a fitting melody for the soul's resting place,
Such a perfect context for the spirit to return to its truth.
So, please, do not plant ice chrysanthemums in my sight,
Let me mourn in the impending bloom of suffering.

I believe some unexperienced encounter of mine
Sits right in this melody,
Perhaps between two notes,
Where I can drink the decay of life,
And also write the legend of love.

The little bird flying from my heart
Is finally made to cry by the lingering touch of the zither.
The ripples of my heart's river destroy the dam of expression,
At this moment, countless poetic thoughts swirl,
But they never quite reach
The sky burial platform of my soul.

枯萎

蕭引漸寂　這穿腸蝕骨
二胡吐露的憂傷
像是走在靈魂深處的鐘錶
刻畫分分秒妙的痛楚

手中的煙燃著　無人在抽
還有比煙燼更純粹的祭奠麼
此刻　形骸虛擬
傷逝　自內心拔節蔓生

誰的手割盡歲月的蒹葭
讓清純的花朵過早在愛情裡嫵媚
並不是沒有芬芳呵
只是被謊言榨幹了水分

攤開的手掌裡　一朵黃玫瑰
站成伊人的模樣　曲終了
餘音將一瓣一瓣蕭瑟收容
我亦坦然這枯萎
不著一詞

Withering

The zither's tone fades into silence,
This pain that gnaws through the marrow,
The sorrow unveiled by the erhu,
Like a clock walking through the depths of the soul,
Marking the exquisite pain of every second.

The cigarette in my hand burns, but no one smokes it.
Is there a purer form of tribute than ash?
At this moment, the body is but a shadow,
Wounds sprout from the heart, twisting and growing.

Whose hand has cut through the years' reeds,
Letting pure flowers bloom too early in the garden of love?
It's not that there's no fragrance,
But rather, the lies have drained the water from their roots.

In the palm of an open hand, a yellow rose,
Standing in the shape of the beloved, the music ends.
The lingering notes collect the petals one by one,
I, too, embrace this withering,
Not a word to speak.

放 生

一

是時候　放生自己
放生這個世界
但需要一場
愈徹底愈芬芳的苦難
還明媚少年給天命
給命裡的毒症
以疼痛的治癒

二

清明　含著紙錢的烏鴉
經過詩人窗前
風雨清白　寒腹清白
在絕境裡打坐的詩人
看見藍色的上帝
正微笑著經過人世的苦難

三

更迭的數字　紛擾的站牌
交錯的線索以及
迷亂的方向之間
一隻尋找骨頭的狗
與掉光羽毛的鷹
狹路相逢在一個
叫做未來的站台

Releasing Life

I

It is time to release myself,
To release this world,
But it requires a suffering,
The more thorough, the more fragrant,
That will return the brightness of youth to fate,
To the poison in my life,
Healing through pain.

II

On Qingming, the crow holding paper money,
Passes by the poet's window.
The wind and rain are pure,
The cold belly is pure.
In the extremity of silence, the poet sits in meditation,
Seeing the blue God,
Smiling as He passes through the world's suffering.

III

The changing numbers, the disordered signposts,
Interwoven clues, and
Confused directions,
Between them, A dog searching for bones,
And an eagle with no feathers,
Meeting on a narrow road at a station
Called the future.

四

眼花了　世界可以折疊
鬢白了　人世少了魅惑
只是一顆背叛了使命的牙
錯投柔腸百結的迷局
讓我身體裡每一個漏洞
都危機四伏

五

以最真實的饑腸
完成對五穀最乾淨的祭祀
以最深沉的疲憊
完成對生命最純粹的禮拜
當我雙手合十
掌心滴落的汗珠裡
一個死去的我背著
一個重生的我

六

風清物明時淨
時間蓮花之上的隱形人
在墓碑上鐫刻人世最溫暖的笑
而我　只能借一塵不染的音符
去敲前世書生的門

IV

When the eyes grow weary, the world can fold,
When the temples turn gray, the world loses its allure.
It's just a tooth that betrayed its mission,
Wrongly thrown into the tangled maze of soft intestines,
And every hole in my body becomes riddled with danger.

V

With the truest hunger,
I offer the cleanest sacrifice to the five grains,
With the deepest fatigue,
I offer the purest worship to life.
When my hands join in prayer,
The sweat drops in my palms,
And a dead me carries
A reborn me.

VI

When the wind is clear and things are bright,
Time becomes a lotus, and the invisible man,
Carves the warmest smile of the world into the tombstone.
And I can only borrow a spotless note,
To knock on the door of a past scholar.

一些預謀之外的情節
——致下山的小和尚

一

除了這預謀的蹈火
以一幕夜色的薄脆
難以承受麥芒之外的命題
雙楠廣福橋西街　今晚
被再次賦予民間的氣質

背叛了夜的意志　街燈
以蕩漾的姿態　靠近煙火
靠近廟堂冷眉　低回的
隱疾和舊傷

人間有了度數的模樣
降B　這陽剛的調性
正好穿透歲月罅隙
直抵男人內心鋒芒的利器
以及最柔軟的盾

Some Unforeseen Plots
—To the Little Monk Descending the Mountain

I

Aside from this premeditated fire-walking,
With the thin crispness of a night scene,
It is hard to bear the proposition
Beyond the wheat ears' edge.
On the West Street of the Double Nan Guangfu Bridge, tonight,
It is once again bestowed with the temperament of the common people.

Having betrayed the will of the night, the streetlights,
With a rippling posture, approach the fireworks,
Approach the cold brows of the temple,
The low murmurs of hidden ailments and old wounds.

Humanity takes on the shape of degrees,
B flat, this masculine tone,
Just right to pierce the gaps in time,
Directly reaching the sharpest tools in a man's heart,
And the softest shields.

二

早被我煙頭一樣掐滅的青春
此刻回到杯中　沉浮或是搖曳
等一場火焰的光　召喚內心
從此萬水千山的趕赴

路過你的人生都成為風景
路過我的風景都成為宿命
今晚　火中取栗的危險
盡我快意

有人期待放下女人肚子裡的包袱
有人期待一口飲盡江湖的魅惑
而我　期待每一次淬火的生命
還能架骨成拐　行走安穩

II

The youth, long extinguished like my cigarette butt,
Now returns to the cup, floating or swaying,
Waiting for the light of a flame to summon the heart,
From then on, rushing toward distant mountains and rivers.

Every life you pass becomes a landscape,
Every landscape I pass becomes fate.
Tonight, the danger of taking chestnuts from the fire,
Is my own indulgence.

Some await the release of the burdens in a woman's belly,
Some long to drink deeply from the charm of the world,
But I, I await every life tempered by fire,
To still build bones and limbs,
And walk steadily.

三

喚醒味蕾懸念的其實是飽滿的果實
一如你撥通的生命通道
羊水洩露花開的訊息
與你有關　也與你無關

只是你一飲而盡的豪邁
正好被趕路的花朵看見
這秘而不宣的默契
值得你手中的酒杯　從此懸空
盛月光　露水和岸邊父親
永不落錨的目光

五年的時光　木魚聲敲醒過往
一圈一圈洇開了輪回
下山的小和尚　誰家香甜的湯茶
讓你流連紅塵　執迷不倦

III

What actually awakens the taste buds' suspense is the ripe fruit,
Just as you dial the life channel,
Amniotic fluid spills out, the flower opens.
It is related to you, and yet unrelated to you.

It is just that your boldness, drinking in one go,
Is seen by the rushing flowers.
This unspoken tacit understanding
Is worth the wine cup in your hand,
Hanging suspended from this point onward,
Holding moonlight, dew, and the father at the shore,
Whose gaze never anchors.

Five years of time, the sound of the wooden fish,
Awakes the past,
Circling, spreading the wheel of reincarnation.
The little monk descending the mountain,
Whose sweet soup and tea,
Made you linger in the world,
Relentlessly attached.

歸 途

一

故鄉不遠 在深蹙的眉梢
在酒杯和腹夜的邊緣 在
一個寫詩男人吞吐的意念之間
可是 孩子 馬蹄落地生根的草原
你先祖心靈睡過的地方
腳步 一定要比音符更輕

孩子請記住 烏鴉或神靈
看護不了我們的家園
濤兒河的水以及青草的香
卻可以洗淨一代又一代
紅塵的憂傷

回家吧 孩子
馬蹄聲裡的鄉愁
早已落地生根

Return Journey

I

The hometown is not far,
At the deep crease of the brow,
At the edge of the wine glass and the belly of the night,
In the thoughts of a man writing poetry.
But, child, the grassland where horse hooves land and take root,
The place where your ancestors' spirits slept,
Your steps must be lighter than the notes of a song.

Child, please remember, Crows or deities
Cannot protect our homeland.
But the waters of Tao'er River and the fragrance of grass
Can cleanse generation after generation
Of the sorrow of worldly dust.

Go home, child,
The homesickness in the sound of hooves
Has long taken root.

二

孩子　在時光睡眠的深處
鄉愁是一尊憂傷的瓷器
回憶愈深　留下的傷痕愈深
你單薄的行囊裝不下疼痛的姓氏
更裝不下　時光深處
那散落成珠　傳奇的榮光

回家吧　孩子
從牧歌裡返回的老馬
馱著你童年的繈褓

馬蹄聲起　馬蹄聲寂
我已不忍卒聽這冷
孩子　回家吧
活在這塵世　更多時候
我們其實只需要
一點單純的暖意
一點家的暖意

II

Child, in the depths of time's sleep,
Homesickness is a sorrowful porcelain vessel.
The deeper the memory, the deeper the wound.
Your thin bag cannot carry the pain of a surname,
Nor the glory of a scattered legend,
Falling like beads in the depths of time.

Go home, child,
The old horse returning from the pastoral song,
Carries the swaddling clothes of your childhood.

The sound of hooves rises,
The sound of hooves falls silent.
I can no longer bear to listen to this cold.
Child, go home,
Living in this world, more often than not,
What we really need
Is just a little pure warmth,
A little warmth of home.

羽落鄉愁

一

冬天最後一朵雪掃淨大地
鷹的翅膀　墊高了天空
高原的孩子　始終堅信
是冰雪世界裡蘇醒的花朵
再一次賦予日頭偉大使命

茶堡河　隱忍淌過時空
像生命潔白的初潮
流經我身體裡的山川河谷
暗礁抑或陰影　註定在
雁鳴洞穿心腸的日子
成為一生最後的流經

火苗點燃的雲朵
那些信仰堆起的石頭
最終都成了思想的頭顱
風回到虛擬　每一次幡動
都有經文傳遞佛的旨意
以及匍匐的靈魂
叩擊在朝聖路上的迴響

Feathers Falling, Homesickness

I

The last snow of winter sweeps the earth clean,
The eagle's wings lift the sky,
The child of the plateau always believes,
It is the flower waking in the icy world
That once again gives the sun its great mission.

Tea Fort River flows silently through time,
Like the pure first tide of life,
Winding through the mountains and valleys inside me,
Reefs or shadows, destined to be
In the days pierced by the call of migrating geese,
Becoming the last stream in a lifetime.

The flames that light up the clouds,
Those stones piled by faith,
In the end, all became the skulls of thought,
The wind returns to the virtual,
With every flutter of the flag,
Scriptures transmit the Buddha's will,
And the crawling souls
Knock in echoes on the pilgrimage road.

二

牛糞火塘裡的火苗
比高原的陽光更乾淨
日子飽滿起來　牛羊
在帳篷外密謀山的另一邊
新鮮欲滴的青草和愛情
並決定把吊鍋煮沸的生活
徹底還給主人

以一枚卵石的姿態
落草似水流年　三十載
一條河別了另一條河
一座山別了另一座山
我別了自己　讓骨頭
遠走高飛

一生都在背誦枝丫上的路
鳥雀們在內心最乾淨的一刻
回到屬自己的天堂
天空還是那麼年輕
怎會在意一隻老去的鷹
卸甲之後　落滿白羽
不忍細讀的鄉愁

II

The flames in the cow dung fire pit
Are cleaner than the plateau's sunlight,
The days grow full, and the cows and sheep
Conspire outside the tent, on the other side of the mountain,
Fresh, dripping grass and love,
Deciding to return the boiling life in the hanging pot
Completely to its owner.

In the shape of a pebble,
Falling like water into the years, thirty years,
One river bids farewell to another river,
One mountain parts with another mountain,
I part with myself, letting my bones
Travel far and soar high.

A lifetime of reciting the road on branches,
The birds return to their own heaven
In the cleanest moment of the heart,
The sky is still so young,
How could it care for an old eagle,
After shedding its armor,
Falling covered in white feathers,
The homesickness too painful to read.

山鷹訴說

一

口銜山風　翅膀裏挾著風暴
這飛翔的精靈不留後路地探訪
止步人類陰謀透明的道場
不屑粉身碎骨的平庸
你目光裡悲憫的深淵
是我獻祭餘生苟且的福祉
我貌似安詳
你桀傲如昔

二

絕壁孤懸　向死而生
怕的不是老去　而是無法結局的傳奇
虛擬了眾生飽食煙火的仰望
把自己逼成雪線之上終極孤獨的飲者
讓不再鋒刃的爪飲恨群峰不屑的蕩漾
讓彎曲的喙直擊逃出生天獵物的戲謔
直至活著的苦難　成為這世間
最不值言說的蒼白

The Mountain Eagle Speaks

I

With its beak grasping the mountain wind,
Wings carry the storm,
This flying spirit visits without leaving a path,
Stopping at the transparent arena of human schemes,
Despising the mediocrity of self-destruction,
In the depths of your gaze, full of pity,
I offer the remains of my life as a sacrifice to a meager fortune,
I appear calm,
But you remain as proud as ever.

II

Cliffside, suspended alone,
Living by the inevitability of death,
Not afraid of aging, but of a legend that cannot be completed,
The virtual reality of beings who have devoured fireworks,
Forcing myself to become the ultimate loner above the snowline,
Letting the claws, no longer sharp, drink the bitterness
Of the contemptuous waves of mountain peaks,
Letting the curved beak strike at the mocking escape of the prey,
Until the suffering of life becomes the pale,
Unworthy thing to speak of in this world.

三

劍芒一般　俯衝而下又仰首而上
絕不多一刻停留　你知道
在飛翔中討活　覷覦人世的暖
是多麼致命的危險　哪怕轉頭的一瞬
你在痛飲的真相裡熱淚盈眶
被你追趕得走投無路的使命
已然還原水鳥般美麗的新娘
燭照　你不折節的風骨

四

迫不及待逃離群山口袋的雛鳥
撞進人間這越收越緊的網
六千米高空　盤旋不墜
始終等不來一紙神諭點亮化身
世事已然滄海桑田　剩下我
如此卑微地愛著這個世界
飽食血肉又在血肉飽滿的現實中
活活餓死自己

III

Like the gleam of a sword,
Diving down and then soaring up again,
Never pausing for even a moment, you know,
In flight, to seek life,
And to covet the warmth of the human world,
Is a dangerous peril,
Even if, in the moment of turning,
You drink deeply of truth, your eyes full of hot tears,
The mission that has chased you into a corner
Is already the beautiful new bride,
Restored like a water bird,
Lit by the candlelight of your unyielding spirit.

IV

Eager to escape the mountain's pocket,
The fledgling bird crashes into the tightening human net,
At 6,000 meters above the ground, spiraling,
Yet never receiving the divine oracle that could light its transformation,
The world has already turned to dust,
And here I remain,
So humble in my love for this world,
Devouring flesh and blood, yet in this blood-soaked reality,
I slowly starve myself.

五

　　我的懷想　你的探訪　透明的牆
　　我看見前世的自己和藍色的父親
　　看見你掉落的每一根羽毛
　　在失血的紙上彙聚成藍色風暴
　　風暴所能抵達的遠方　理想和信仰
　　都將在光陰最初的血液裡復活
　　而我們　只在文字燃燒的灰燼裡
　　彼此　安葬

V

My nostalgia, your visit, the transparent wall,
I see my past self and my blue father,
I see every feather you drop,
Gathering into a blue storm on the paper of blood,
The distance the storm can reach: ideals and faith,
Will all be resurrected in the earliest blood of time,
And we, Only in the ashes of the words we burned,
Will bury each other.

隱喻的詞根

一

凌晨六點　銀河路
路燈隨晨霧蕩漾的迷途
陀螺聲回蕩在彼岸
保潔工人的掃帚
上學孩童的單車
攜清光途經這人間尋常
乘金屬火焰出發的我
背著自己的倒影
背著一生清白

二

星月凝眸　一朵雲
就是撫慰靈魂的袈裟
命運銜痛　一座山
就是慈航普渡的世尊
螻蟻仰望的草
隱在花叢緘默
花叢仰望的喬木
沉於樓影肅立
有人以瞑目重釋春序
我讓埋在心裡的雷
終生靜默

The Roots of Metaphor

I

At six in the morning, on Galaxy Road,
Streetlights sway in the mist of morning fog, lost paths,
The sound of a spinning top echoes on the other shore,
A janitor's broom,
A child's bicycle on the way to school,
All passing through this mundane world, carrying the light.
I set off, fueled by metallic flames,
Carrying my own reflection,
Carrying a lifetime of innocence.

II

Stars and moon gaze back, a cloud,
It is the robe that soothes the soul,
Destiny, in pain, a mountain,
It is the Buddha's mercy, ferrying souls to safety.
The ants gaze upward at the grass,
Hidden silently in the flowers,
The flowers gaze upward at the trees,
Sinking in the shadow of buildings, standing solemnly.
Some close their eyes to interpret the season of spring,
I let the thunder buried in my heart
Remain silent for life.

三

當苦難以勾魂的曼妙
當饑荒以隔世的癢
當崇高以茹毛的殤
荒誕以荒誕正名
滑稽以滑稽面具

誰在盜用春天的名義
讓我無顏接近　一枚
把大地舉重若輕的詞根

四

拋開這失貞的肉體
在中毒未深的骨殖上
寫一些水火相容的音符
這量子對撞的神奇流體
在我漏洞百出的身體
逼出隱疾　暗礁
以及變節的頌詞

多年前的一次誕生
梵音起　隕星落
這註定無法圓滿的修行
每一場劫　都是一次癌變

III

When suffering unfolds in the allure of the soul,
When famine itches like a distant memory,
When nobility is a wound that eats raw,
Absurdity is named by absurdity,
Comedy dons the mask of farce.

Who is using the name of spring without permission,
Preventing me from approaching, a root
That lifts the earth effortlessly?

IV

Throwing aside this forsaken body,
On the unpoisoned bone marrow,
I write notes that are both fire and water,
The miraculous fluid of quantum collisions,
Emerging from my flawed body,
Forcing out hidden ailments, reefs,
And the hymns of betrayal.

Many years ago, there was a birth,
The sound of a chant began, a falling star,
This journey, destined to remain incomplete,
Every disaster, a metamorphosis.

母親的江山

七十九的老母
硬生生　用相互磨損的膝蓋骨
換取繼續行走的權利
這些年　忍住不喊的疼痛
都擠在枯樹皮般的臉上

成為孤兒的那一年
十四歲就接過獨自討活的擔子
單薄的小身子　掙脫黃土的泥濘
頭也不回去了高原
一走　就是三十年

不問出身的高原
低頭　是唯一被俯允的姿態
背一個兜一個牽一個
爬坡上坎　穿林涉穀
姐弟仨的童年
都在你一人身上行走

本是飛鳥走獸的領地
匍匐才能躲避的風刀霜劍
挑起一家五口的你　只能
用單薄的身子硬生生接住
卑微　卻義無反顧

Mother's Kingdom

At seventy-nine, my old mother
Fights on, using the grinding of her knee joints
To earn the right to continue walking.
All these years, the pain she has held back
Has gathered in the withered skin of her face.

The year I became an orphan,
At fourteen, I took up the burden of surviving alone.
A frail little body, pulling free from the mud of the earth,
I didn't look back as I climbed to the plateau,
A journey that would last for thirty years.

The plateau, with no questions about origin,
Bows its head, the only posture it allows.
With one hand holding, one arm carrying,
I climb up hills, cross forests and valleys.
The childhood of my siblings and me,
Was carried by you alone.

This was once the land of birds and beasts,
But now the wind's blade and frost's sword
Could only be avoided by crawling.
You, who carried the weight of a family of five,
Could only use your frail body to bear it,
Humbly, but without hesitation.

无精打采的油灯
像有魔法的倦眼
催眠小木屋　即使夜深
永远洞开的柴门　也不忘
给屋外蜷缩一地的月光
留一点火塘的余温
烘乾山里人的日子
月色一般清凉
针线一般密实

三十年　写进你骨髓里的
不只命运的冷　光阴的镑
更有无法倒叙余罪的灰
变形的双腿　弯曲的脊柱
让你离地心引力越来越近
近得只差一次心跳

终于可以没有负累的行走
你却已经负担不起
缊袄袋一样鼓鼓囊囊

又空又轻的身体
拐杖忠诚　知道你
每一步都用尽了全力
阳光就在窗外
蓝天就在屋顶上
公园就在马路对面
你知道这大好春光里

The oil lamp, listless,
Like a weary eye with magical powers,
Hypnotizes the little wooden house. Even deep into the night,
The ever-open door of the cabin never forgets
To leave a little warmth from the fire pit,
To dry the days of the people in the mountains.
The moonlight is as cool as water,
The sewing thread, tight and fine.

Thirty years have been written into your bones,
Not only the cold of fate, the rust of time,
But also the grayness of unspoken sins.
Deformed legs and a bent spine
Draw you closer to the earth's gravity,
So close that only one more heartbeat separates you.

Finally, you can walk without burden,
But you can no longer bear
The heavy load of life,
As if your body, light and empty,
Has become a swaddling bag, full of air.

The cane is loyal, knowing that
With every step, you exert your last ounce of strength.
The sunshine is just outside the window,
The blue sky is right on the roof,
The park is just across the street,
You know that in this great springtime,

溢滿花朵蜜汁的空氣
可以給你一些生活的甜頭
可一道戒備森嚴的門
總是讓你望而生畏

沒力氣孤獨了
一個人的時候　你習慣
和彩電冰箱洗衣機說話
當然偶爾也說給另一個
遠在天國的人

The air is full of the sweet fragrance of flowers,
Offering you a taste of life's sweetness.
But a tightly guarded door
Always makes you tremble.

There is no strength left for loneliness.
When you are alone, you get used to
Talking to the TV, the fridge, the washing machine.
Of course, occasionally, you also speak to another,
Far away in heaven.

先生 此别

一

以眼淚之輕 承載生離死別的重
以肉體之輕 沐染煙火之上的香
此刻 我置身四十二米半空
眺望人間燈火 安瀾如昨

二

承背負之重 舉黎庶之尊 築浮生之夢
俯身親煙火 仰首聽風吟
淺謀如讖 雲漢已邈
再讀人間 已是火光中掣筆 燭焰裡沉香

三

低入塵埃 我們仰望暗夜啟明
隱入塵煙 我們敬慕孤勇逆行
與百姓共風雨的肩 才能擋住
歷史的灰與信仰的荒

Farewell, Sir

I

With the lightness of tears, I bear the weight of parting and death
With the lightness of flesh, I bathe in the fragrance above mortal smoke
At this moment, I stand suspended in the forty-two-meter sky
Gazing at the mortal lights, calm as they ever were

II

Bearing the weight of burdens, upholding the dignity of the people, forging dreams of a fleeting life
Bending low to kiss the mortal smoke, lifting my head to hear the wind sing
Shallow plans prove prophetic, the Milky Way fades into the far distance
To read the world again
Is to wield a brush amid flames, to let agarwood linger in candlelight

III

Bow low to the dust, we look up for the dawn in the dark night
Fade into the mortal smoke, we admire the lone courage of those who march against the tide
Only shoulders that share wind and rain with the people Can block
The ash of history and the desolation of faith

四

以赤子之心錨定光陰憔悴
待空穀鳥鳴喚醒惶惑人間
而鳥盡的林子　藏弓如淵
兔死的荒丘　走狗競歡

五

聽山河嗚咽　吞盡悲壯隱喻
看星月垂淚　打濕弦外晨光
空盞獨飲　　微醺之後
我是自己卑微的草民
亦是自己居高的大王
待我像一支煙燃盡熱血
先生　此別

IV

With a childlike heart, I anchor the haggard passage of time
Waiting for birdsong in the empty valley to rouse the confused world
Yet in the forest where birds are gone,
bows are hidden like an abyss
On the barren mound where hares lie dead,
hounds revel in their triumph

V

Hear the mountains and rivers sob, swallowing all metaphors of heroism and sorrow
See the stars and moon shed tears, dampening the morning light beyond the melody
Drinking alone from an empty cup, after a light haze of drunkenness
I am my own humble commoner
And also my own exalted king
When I burn away my blood like a cigarette
Farewell, Sir

第二輯

突圍的另一種可能性

Volume II:

Another Possibility of Breaking Through

所 見

枝條上逗留片刻的冰花兒
或是覆蓋原野最初的雪花兒
帶著一塵不染的神諭
受命的蓓蕾或是嫩芽
衝破寒冷意志地封鎖
你所見新生　便是自己的新生

一隻小鳥留在雪地上的使命
淒絕的冷芒直抵你的內心
寒腹或是迷途的彷徨
無根的大雪消弭所有真相
你看見的尋覓仍沿著愛的方向
你心裡的溫暖　即是眾生的溫暖

一粒冰花兒的消融
破解一條溪流曲折的輪回
一粒雪花兒的消融
揭秘一座山頭隱忍的修行
和懸崖一起陷入沉思的樹木
找到另一種生長的方向

雪線以外　無名小草
舉起的天空倒影匍匐的眾生
煙火之外　冰雪結成的花兒
折射的光　照亮諸神趕路的背影
至剛亦至柔　至真亦至幻
一念萬物生　一念淨寂滅

What is Seen

The ice flowers resting briefly on the branches,
Or the first snowflakes covering the fields,
Carrying an untarnished oracle,
The appointed bud or tender sprout,
Breaking through the cold resolve's blockade,
What you see as rebirth is your own rebirth.

A small bird's mission left in the snow,
The desolate cold light piercing your heart,
A cold belly or the uncertainty of a lost path,
The rootless snow erases all truths.
What you see, searching, still follows the direction of love,
The warmth in your heart is the warmth of all beings.

The melting of an ice flower,
Unlocking the winding cycle of a stream,
The melting of a snowflake,
Revealing the hidden practice of a mountain's summit,
The trees, pondering with the cliff,
Find another direction of growth.

Beyond the snow line, nameless grasses,
Lift their sky-reflecting shadows—crawling beings,
Beyond the fireworks, flowers formed of ice and snow,
Reflected light illuminating the gods' hurried steps,
The hardest and the softest, the truest and the illusory,
With a single thought, all things come into being;

而我　是一粒被風刮走
鐫刻高原姓氏　血肉飽滿的籽
拎著油燈尋覓溫暖的火塘
可脆弱的都市
接不住一粒雪降下的福祉
油燈將滅　火塘將冷
當裸露的根鬚掛滿冰花兒一樣
易碎的念想　我眼裡的眾生
高蹈於塵埃之上的蕩漾
提前洞開人生結局

如是　我們彼此看見
如在一粒冰雪結成的花兒裡
看見整個世界以及世界之外

With a single thought, they are purified and extinguished.
And I am but a grain blown away by the wind,
Carving the surname of the plateau, a seed full of flesh and blood,
Carrying an oil lamp in search of a warm hearth,
But fragile cities
Cannot receive the blessings of a single falling snowflake.
The oil lamp will extinguish, the hearth will grow cold,
When exposed roots are adorned with ice flowers,
The fragile thoughts—the beings in my eyes,
Dancing above the dust,
Already withered, the end of life laid bare in advance.

Thus, we see each other,
As if in a snowflake-formed flower,
Seeing the entire world, and beyond the world.

關於夏花的沉吟與獨白

一 生如夏花

這個夏天　開得再美的花
也不流一滴汗
南中國濱海　花兒結滿天堂鳥的表情
流出紅色的淚

詩歌柔軟心跳鍍亮的一方天宇
《安魂曲》裡花香四溢
不說蒙愛吧　靈魂的居所
花開是殤　花謝亦殤

佔據一縷花香　飛躍生命的暗傷
生如夏花　與其風情萬種地臨世
不若輕靈絕塵地飛翔

On the Murmurs and Soliloquies of Summer Flowers

I. Life as Summer Flowers

This summer, no matter how beautifully the flowers bloom,
They do not shed a single drop of sweat.
Along the southern shores of China, the flowers
Carry the expressions of heaven's birds,
Pouring out red tears.

Poetry softens the heartbeat, casting a shining sky,
In the "Requiem," the fragrance of flowers fills the air,
Not to say "beloved," but the soul's dwelling,
For the bloom is a sorrow, and the wither is also sorrow.

Occupying a wisp of fragrance,
Leaping over life's dark wounds,
Life is like summer flowers—
Better to soar lightly, transcendent,
Than to stay and charm the world with its myriad beauty.

二　溫暖來自黑夜

鋪紙為床　捉筆寫夢的日子
你是受戒的僧侶
於一紙青燈打坐　詩卷壘塚
於一枚瘦筆入定　才思鑄碑
獨自守夜的人　用背影囚禁自己
等待信仰與遺言匯合的一天
從詩歌出發　最終回到詩歌
只是為了不讓心靈背井離鄉

兄弟呵　白晝空曠得聽不到回聲
溫暖來自黑夜　正好收心為徒
堅持做一粒開花的石頭吧
並以此祝禱和祭祀活著的每一天

II. Warmth Comes from the Night

Paper laid as a bed, catching a pen to write dreams,
You are the monk receiving vows,
Sitting beneath a blue lantern,
Stacks of poetry built like a mound,
A slender pen entering deep meditation,
thoughts chiseling into stone.
The one who guards the night,
Imprisons himself with his own shadow,
Waiting for the day when faith and final words merge.
From poetry we start, and ultimately return to poetry,
Only to prevent the soul from being exiled.

Brother, the day is so vast, it does not echo.
Warmth comes from the night,
Just right to gather the heart as a disciple.
Persist in being a flower-blooming stone,
And with this, offer prayers and sacrifices for every day that we live.

三　沉默　是痛醒的語言

我們的耳朵聆聽了太多的不幸
讓嘴休息吧　以善良的名義
現在討論　流淚的蚌殼是否
遺失了胎結的珍珠
真的了無意義
別再試圖對著天空禱告
飛翔著的　除了精靈還有盜賊
即使不能　頓悟於死亡的陰霾
也請寬恕每一個被文字咬傷的人

吞咽麥芒的人　流落他鄉
懷抱詩歌的光芒　早已病入膏肓
且允許饑餓的風在啃食落葉之後
沉默地陷入一粒石頭的心事

III. Silence, the Language of Waking Pain

We have listened to too much misfortune,
Let the mouth rest—by the name of kindness.
Now, let us discuss whether the tearful clam
Has lost the pearl formed within.
Really, it holds no meaning.
Stop attempting to pray to the sky.
Flying in the air, besides spirits, there are also thieves.
Even if we cannot awaken to the shadow of death,
Let us forgive every soul bitten by words.

Those who swallow the wheat stalks,
Wander far from home,
Embracing the glow of poetry, already sick to the core.
And allow the hungry winds to devour fallen leaves,
Silently sinking into the heart of a stone's thoughts.

秋天適宜安放的調性

一

驚蟬的叫聲留在了某個清晨
這個秋天我已不打算逐一盤點
憂傷溺而無影的黃昏
單翅的倦鴉撲騰的一方
我不忍凝目　一楨枯樹
連最後的影子也丟了

失聰　在月桂的芬芳鳴囀秋水之前
失明　在落紅的疼痛敲打瘦土之前
不說愛憎　不說悲喜
更別試著從記憶的樹上摘取
一串熟透的葡萄
使童貞蒙難

The Tone Suited for Autumn's Rest

I

The startled cicada's cry remains in some morning,
This autumn, I have no intention of reviewing each detail.
Sorrow drowns, its shadowless dusk,
A lone-winged, weary crow flutters across the sky,
I cannot bear to fix my gaze,
Even the last shadow is lost on a bare tree.

Deafness, before the bay laurel's fragrant song stirs the autumn waters.
Blindness, before the pain of falling petals strikes the thin earth.
I shall speak of neither love nor hate,
Neither joy nor sorrow,
Nor attempt to pick from the memory's tree
A cluster of ripened grapes,
To make the virgin suffer.

二

所有的隕落和殘缺都與名譽無關
只證實了一種命運
秋風在丟失激情以後　飽含愛意
蠶食也就正名為撫慰
而我內心殘缺的一頁
需要一次酣釅的霜降　救贖
秋天的晨光和夕輝
已不再是色誘　觸之即沒的性格
像極了一次煙火外的愛情
蘇醒在骨子裡流浪的宿結
原本不關愛情的短長

II

All falls and fractures have nothing to do with reputation,
They only confirm one destiny:
The autumn wind, after losing its passion, fills with love,
Devouring itself, which then redefines as comfort.
And one missing page in my heart
Needs a thorough frost to redeem it.
The morning light and evening glow of autumn
No longer tempt,
Touching them is no longer a fleeting trait,
Like a love outside of fireworks,
Awakened in the wandering past of my bones,
Which never concerned itself with the length of love.

三

秋意沉澱得已經很深了
葉叢花間偶爾一勺輕顫的蝶影
遺留的淒美　比初雪還涼
淋濕夢境的　不是巴山的夜雨
而是漂泊者提前預約的一段光陰

殉死的白馬　因戀上了歌唱
連魂魄都被塵世流放
自高處散落的詩句
落進凝望者的杯盞
正好作釀　煮夢

III

The autumn spirit has already deeply settled.
Among the leaves and flowers, occasionally a butterfly's tremor,
The beauty left behind is colder than the first snow,
Not the night rain of Bashan wetting the dreams,
But rather a period of time prearranged by a wanderer.

The dying white horse, because it fell in love with singing,
Even its soul was exiled by the dust of the world.
The verses scattered from high above,
Fall into the gazer's cup,
Just enough to brew and dream.

四

佇傯一握　秋河瘦在我的五指間
一夜白頭的蘆葦　與岸作最後的道別
鬱鬱而行的季節　輾轉於一枚落葉
懷抱詩歌的光芒　我也輾轉
鍍滿季節滄桑　一段
無法回頭的岸

天堂的聖燈　竊取了人間早熟的語言
行走在上的兄弟　以我貧瘠的胸膛
收藏你的腳印　並非是想步你後塵
適合憑弔的季節　也適合夢回
做那追趕水中太陽的玩童吧
而不是聖燈裡飛翔的青鳥

IV

In a fleeting grasp, autumn's river thins between my fingers,
The reeds, turning white overnight, bid their final farewell to the shore.
The season, slowly moving, revolves around a fallen leaf,
Embracing the light of poetry, I also turn,
Coated with the wear of seasons,
A stretch of shore I can never return to.

The sacred light of heaven has stolen the world's early words,
Brothers walking beneath it, with my barren chest,
I collect your footprints,
Not because I wish to follow in your steps.
This season, fit for mourning,
Is also fit for dreams,
To be that child chasing the sun in the water,
Not the bluebird flying in the sacred light.

天命辭
——致自己

一　背手

半生虛空
徒留一枚軀殼
背手　以此
攥緊餘生

二　線索

一退再退的髮際線
讓向陽而生成為悖論
須髯賁張　埋置線索
垂釣來世懸念

三　角度

倒立
才發現
雙腳留下所有印記
只為靠近天堂

The Farewell to Destiny

— *A Letter to Myself*

I. Hands Behind My Back

Half a life of emptiness,
Only a shell remains,
With my hands behind my back,
I hold tightly to what little remains of my life.

II. Clues

The retreating hairline,
Makes the sun's direction a paradox.
A mustache brims forth, laying out clues,
Fishing for the uncertainties of the next life.

III. Perspective

Inverting myself,
I realize
All the marks left by my feet,
Were made only to approach heaven.

四　燃燒

每深吸一口
就發現自己燃燒得愈來愈快
其實　根本不需要煙
只是用盡半生
也沒找到點燃自己的方式

五　止語

半生與文字為敵
是時候和解
餘生只與一個字
廝守始終

六　胎死

越來越慈祥的
不是我的面容
而是眼袋和皺紋裡
胎死的光陰

IV. Burning

With each deep breath,
I find myself burning faster and faster,
Truth is, no smoke is needed,
I've used half a life,
But still haven't found the way to ignite my own soul.

V. Silence

Half a life in battle with words,
It's time for reconciliation,
For the rest of my life,
I will live with only one word,
Bound to it forever.

VI. Miscarried Life

What grows more benevolent
Is not my face,
But the bags under my eyes,
And the time in them,
The unborn life.

七　決裂

天命之後
適合與自己徹底決裂
讓掙脫袈裟的靈魂
向死而生

八　悲涼

悲涼是一個多肉的詞根
承受不起太多水分
而酒的醇烈
是我們骨子裡需要的陽光

九　健忘

健忘　其實是
從出生就開始有的
此後我想遺忘的來世
被你們叫做天堂

VII. Break

After destiny,
It's time to sever ties with myself completely,
Let the soul, freed from its cloak,
Live to die.

VIII. Melancholy

Melancholy is a word-root rich with flesh,
Unable to bear too much moisture,
Yet the strong wine,
Is the sunlight we need in our bones.

IX. Forgetfulness

Forgetfulness, in truth,
Is something we are born with,
And so I wish to forget the next life,
Which you call heaven.

十　清明的雨

清明的雨還是如期
下在古人的詩句裡
多年前　我穿過風雨而來
不帶一絲悲傷

十一　揉沙

所有塵世的沙
都長成眼中的桃花
我油然而生的悲憫
無關沙的原罪以及桃花的殤
而是骨子裡的卑微

十二　演

把自己演得像別人
是演技
把自己演得像自己
是修行

X. Clear Rain

The clear rain still falls,
On the ancient verses of the poets,
Many years ago, I passed through the storm,
Without a trace of sorrow.

XI. Kneading Sand

All the sand of the world
Grows into peach blossoms in my eyes,
The sympathy that rises in me
Has nothing to do with the original sin of sand, nor the sorrow of peach blossoms,
But rather, the humility in my bones.

XII. Acting

To act like someone else
Is mere skill,
To act like yourself
Is true practice.

十三　官場

黯黑的潛臺詞　以及
聚光燈下燦爛的深淵
一些明媚的面具
一群蹈火的飛蛾

十四　謝幕

有人帶走自己交還上帝
有人被別人帶走
蓋子一旦揭開　穿幫
便再無法成為謝幕的理由
而我　只是雙手捂緊
人間四月冷暖　沉默的觀眾

十五　天命

而立　劍走偏鋒
不惑　長纓問鼎
天命　一張驚弓
一盞液態火焰
一把待發老骨

XIII. The Official World

The dark undertones,
And the brilliant abyss under the spotlight,
Bright masks,
A group of moths flying into the flame.

XIV. The Curtain Falls

Some return themselves to God,
Others are taken away by others,
Once the lid is lifted, the disguise is torn,
There's no more reason to close the curtain,
And I, Just press my hands tightly together,
A silent observer of the warmth and cold of April.

XV. Destiny

At thirty, I take the path less traveled,
At forty, I reach for the sword's hilt,
Destiny,
A startled bowstring,
A lantern of liquid flame,
An old bone ready to release its arrow.

十六　少年和鷹

天很空　山很靜
煙火很輕　雲朵很沉
山坳木屋裡的小少年
梨花金頂的鷹
出山的小少年將遠行
鷹的翅膀便擦亮天空
他們曾經共同生活在
靈魂做的窩裡

十七　兵器和樂器

不動聲色躺在紙上的文字
是我奇門遁甲的冷兵器
至於這一身骨頭
並不是我的利刃
而是樂器　我只想
彈一地錚然
或大道若水

十八　靈魂的夢境

總有一段月光
忍不住溜進我的房間
我想　應該是受了
煙火或酒香的誘惑
而他們都來自
靈魂與夢境深處

XVI. The Boy and the Eagle

The sky is vast, the mountains quiet,
The fireworks are light, the clouds heavy,
A young boy in the mountain hut,
A hawk with pearly white wings,
The boy who leaves the mountain will journey far,
The eagle's wings will polish the sky,
Once they both lived together in
A nest made of souls.

XVII. Weapons and Instruments

The words, lying quietly on paper,
Are my cold weapons of magical strategy.
As for this body,
It's not my blade,
But an instrument,
I only wish to play a resounding sound,
Or perhaps a grand, watery path.

XVIII. Dreams of the Soul

There's always a moment when the moonlight
Can't help but slip into my room,
I think it must have been
Tempted by the fragrance of fireworks or wine,
For they both come from
The depths of the soul and dreams.

十九　戰爭與賜予

天命　掐指一算
與三個女人年齡集合的數差
正好是十四小少年出山之時
行囊裡所有與山有關的賜予
便是餘生與三個女人對峙的
秘密武器

二十　落葉

這些樹
在窗外站了很久
除了鳥兒殷勤探訪
它們幾乎一動不動

我也在窗前坐了很久
記不清　哪一座
被風搬走的山頭
葬了少年的我
如今只剩下落葉
鋪開我的敘世

噓　又一片落葉
擊中我的肋骨
我把疼痛
還給了風

XIX. War and Bestowals

Destiny, I calculate it,
The difference in the age of three women,
Is exactly when the young boy leaves the mountain.
In my bag, all the gifts related to the mountain
Are my secret weapons
for facing the three women in the future.

XX. Fallen Leaves

These trees
Have stood outside my window for a long time,
Apart from the birds' frequent visits,
They remain almost still.

I too have sat by the window for a long time,
Unclear which mountain,
Once carried away by the wind,
Has buried the youth within me.
Now only fallen leaves remain,
Spreading my narrative.

Hush, another leaf falls,
Striking my ribs,
I return the pain
Back to the wind.

折春記

一

剛出娘胎　不會寫字的她
以啼哭為柬　預約立春
次日便叩窗而來
她卻在屋裡垂淚
戴著偌大一隻口罩
春天會不會認不出她

二

窗外　覓食的麻雀
予女兒自由的啟示
她把圖畫本悄悄挪近陽臺
看陽光一寸寸
照亮筆下的房子

三

我對困於屋內的女兒說
是門窗鎖了自由
她轉身就給畫裡的房子
添上一對翅膀

Folding Spring

I

Fresh from her mother's womb, she cannot write a word
Her cry is an invitation, booking the Start of Spring
It taps at the window the next day
Yet she weeps inside the room
Beneath an oversized mask
Will Spring fail to recognize her?

II

Outside the window, sparrows forage for food
Granting her daughter a revelation of freedom
She quietly moves her sketchbook near the balcony
Watching sunlight, inch by inch
Light up the house beneath her pen

III

To my daughter, trapped indoors, I say
It is the doors and windows that lock away freedom
She turns, and at once to the house in her drawing
Adds a pair of wings

四

當我寫下這些文字
院子裡的斑鳩和小精靈
距我不足兩米
讀文字裡的善意與懺悔
也讀牆角　歸不了故土
一粒種子遠眺的憂傷

五

當悲傷漫過所有白牆
空曠暴露城市的心跳
女兒把畫紙輕輕對折
說要把這個無辜的春天
藏進折痕裡

六

口罩與奶嘴
一歲煖朵不問而取
她天命之年的父親
卻困在　牛奶麵包與消毒水
誰更貼近活著真相的迷局裡
迷了路

IV

As I write these words
Turtledoves and sprites in the yard
Are less than two meters from me
They read the kindness and remorse in the lines
And also the sorrow
Of a seed by the wall, far from its homeland, staring into the distance

V

When grief overflows all white walls
Emptiness bares the city's heartbeat
My daughter folds the drawing paper gently
Saying she will tuck this innocent spring
Into the crease

VI

Mask and pacifier
One-year-old Xuanduo takes without asking
Her father, in his fiftieth year
Is trapped in a maze
Wondering which draws closer to the truth of living:
Milk and bread, or disinfectant
Lost in the labyrinth

七

鳳凰木如孔雀展屏
桂花樹立似撐傘少女
多好的時節　生靈皆飽蘸春的生機
唯有枝丫晾曬的口罩
讓歸巢的鳥兒　不安地徘徊

八

庚子正月十三　大吉日
抬頭喜見日月同輝
卻只隔一個頭顱的距離
我慌忙捂緊口罩
食指輕豎唇間

九

本該爛漫的春色
翻過院牆　便已枯萎
我想托自由的野鴿
吹響哨音
叫停上帝翻牌的手

VII

The flamboyant tree fans its leaves like a peacock's tail
The sweet osmanthus tree stands like a maiden holding an umbrella
What a fine season—all living things brim with spring's vitality
Only the masks hanging to dry on the branches
Make the homecoming birds
Pace about, uneasy

VIII

The thirteenth day of the first lunar month, Gengzi Year, an auspicious day
I look up, glad to see the sun and moon shine together
Yet they are only a head's distance apart
I hurry to press my mask tight
And place my index finger lightly on my lips

IX

The spring scenery that should have been bright and blooming
Wilts the moment it climbs over the courtyard wall
I want to entrust a free wild pigeon
To blow its whistle
And stop the hand of God that flips the cards

有關驢的隱喻

一　愛上被殺的感覺

桅杆坡　一頭即將被殺的驢
磨槽裡躺滿溫暖的遺言
心裡無數次泛起的刀光
遠在引頸就戮前

但他還是那麼珍惜
眼前這燦爛的陽光
幻想著　在去另一個世界之前
把這裡的黑夜變得明亮起來

一頭喜歡幹活兒的驢
愛上被殺的感覺
這要了老命的隱喻
顛覆了誰的秩序

Metaphor of the Donkey

I. Loving the Feeling of Being Killed

At the mast hill, a donkey, soon to be slaughtered,
Lies in the grinding trough, filled with warm last words.
Countless flashes of knives rise in its heart,
Far ahead, its neck is stretched for the killing.

But it still cherishes
The brilliant sunlight before it.
It fantasizes that, before going to another world,
It will make the night here bright.

A donkey who loves hard work,
Falls in love with the feeling of being killed.
This fatal metaphor,
Subverts whose order?

二　以驢的名義

寧折不屈的半生
終於到了謝罪天命的時候
沒什麼可呈堂的供狀
不吭聲原本是驢最大的美德

慨然引頸　提前打開結局
從悲劇中站立起來的驢
留下醒世的預言
狼吃肉　卻賦予殺戮最大的虔敬
作為鳥　鷹總是抓起山頭飛行
傲骨險於反骨　何必言忠
天國的人只落下凝固的笑
香火已冷　人倫已杳

奉老育幼討生活的人們
誰又不是挺直了腰板
給老天跪下　至於那些
作祟人間的面具
不過是上帝痛快後
扔下的擦手紙

II. In the Name of the Donkey

A life spent with unyielding stubbornness,
Finally reaches the time to apologize to fate.
No written confession to present,
Silent obedience was once the donkey's greatest virtue.

With a resolute neck,
It opens the ending in advance.
The donkey that rises from tragedy
Leaves behind a warning for the world:
The wolf eats meat but gives the highest reverence to slaughter,
As a bird, the eagle always takes flight from the mountaintop.
Pride is more dangerous than rebellion—why speak of loyalty?
Those in heaven only leave behind frozen smiles,
The incense has gone cold, humanity is gone.

For those who raise the old and care for the young,
Who among them doesn't stand tall,
Kneeling before Heaven? As for those
Masks that plague the world,
They are merely the paper used by God after pleasure,
Cast aside like a napkin.

突圍的另一種可能性

一

我在一扇門外　聽見心跳
不是我自己的
屋裡沒人

門不會代替主人發出邀請
我轉身　遠赴的下一個春天
沒有門檻

正好　枝頭有落葉飄降
這是一封請柬
送達在我枯萎的前一秒

如果　無可選擇
註定要踏著落葉前行
我將徹底忘記自己的心跳

Another Possibility of Breaking Out

I.

I stand outside a door, listening to a heartbeat—
Not my own.
Inside, no one.

The door will not invite in its master.
I turn away, heading toward the next spring,
One without thresholds.

Just in time, a leaf falls from the branch—
A letter,
delivered in the final second before I wither.

If there is no choice,
Destined to walk on the fallen leaves,
I will forget my heartbeat completely.

二

很多日子　我蟄伏如蠱
我的歌聲並不清涼
周遭的樹葉卻一天比一天綠

兩年了　這可不是一隻蠱的壽命
所以　當我停止歌唱的時候
枝頭滾落最後一滴汗
就是我的絕唱

我的夥伴　一隻被槍聲驚飛
一隻被天籟勾了魂兒
還有一隻　開始學會
做秋涼以後的準備

他們都是大師
可以享受孤獨
而我　六根不淨的小僧
經不住一粒小小病毒的侵蝕

II

For many days, I've hidden like a silkworm,
My song is not fresh or cool.
But the leaves around me grow greener each day.

Two years have passed,
This is not the lifespan of a silkworm.
So, when I stop singing,
The last drop of sweat falls from the branch—
That will be my swan song.

My companions: One, startled by the sound of gunshots,
One, enchanted by celestial voices,
And another, beginning to prepare for the autumn cool.

They are all masters—
Able to embrace solitude.
But I, a novice with impure senses,
Am overwhelmed by a small virus's invasion.

三

不是我學會了安靜
生活的細節容不得突圍
縱使輕盈如詩歌的翅膀
又怎能飛越弱水三千的堅硬

內心沒有輪回
因為詩歌　昨天我還是個孩子
今天就已經老了
徒剩時光飲恨

思想的蟲子　總是在黑夜
啃噬我的骨頭
和我一起糜爛的
是一些回聲結出的果實

靈魂失語的時候
詩歌　正被生活的詞典刪除
無限放大的空洞
收容我卑微的涅槃

III

It is not that I have learned to be quiet,
But the details of life leave no space to break free.
Even with wings as light as poetry,
How can one fly beyond the unyielding,
Three thousand miles of hard waters?

No reincarnation within me,
For yesterday, I was still a child,
Today, I am already old—
Only time remains, bitter with regret.

The worm of thought,
Gnaws at my bones in the night,
And together with me, rots—
The fruits of echoes, ripening.

When the soul falls silent,
Poetry is being erased from life's dictionary.
An infinitely expanding void
Holds my humble rebirth.

高處，鷹在言說

一　背景　清冽長笛

高原把胸膛打開　捧出了大山
大山把胸膛打開　捧出的男人叫漢子
捧出的女人　她還是女人
野百合一樣的女人

野百合一樣的女人和她的漢子
從大山胸膛裡捧出春天
讓從不結果的雪花　以光芒的形式
烙印成我靈魂的胎記

拽著父親的背影上山頂
我看見　很多鳥的翅膀
將一朵又一朵雲劃傷以後
天空開始流淌蔚藍的血液
我還看見　比時間的回聲還悠遠
雪野蒼茫的憂傷

背著母親　走出木屋以遠
我想尋找　童話裡療傷的梅花鹿
以及閃電般掠過雪原的火狐
我渴望學會它們的奔跑
讓幼小的夢想
跑出群山的口袋

The Eagle Speaking from Above

I. Background - Clear Flute

The plateau opens its chest, presenting the mountains.
The mountains open their chest, and the man they produce is
called a hero.
The woman they produce, she remains a woman,
A wild lily of a woman.

A wild lily of a woman and her hero
Bring forth spring from the mountain's chest,
Letting the snowflakes, which never bear fruit,
Imprint their form on my soul as radiant marks.

Grasping my father's silhouette, I climb to the summit,
I see the wings of many birds
Carving through the clouds,
As the sky begins to bleed blue.
I also see, beyond the echo of time,
The sorrow of the snow-covered wilderness.

Carrying my mother, walking away from the cabin,
I yearn to find the healing deer from fairy tales,
And the fire fox darting across the snowy plains.
I long to learn their way of running,
To let my small dreams
Escape from the pouch of the mountains.

二 印記 沉鬱大提琴

奔跑的樹跌倒　爬起來
站成另一顆樹
落下一地鳥聲
奔跑的山跌倒　爬起來
站成另一座山
落下一地飛翔的影子

我在自己的幻覺裡奔跑
麻雀的視線與我平行
鷹在高處譏笑我
比雲朵還軟弱的理想

從最後的幻覺中站起來
我站成另一個自己
站成一個漢子
我肆意放開喉嚨
大喊一嗓子　遠山有雪
簌簌而落

小木屋長成了記憶的化石
跌落的鳥聲以及飛翔的影子
卻一直在我的生命裡盤旋
像一把大提琴
沉鬱地穿透時空

II. Imprint - Melancholic Cello

The running tree falls, then rises
To become another tree,
Leaving a ground full of bird calls.
The running mountain falls, then rises
To become another mountain,
Leaving behind flying shadows.

I run within my own illusion,
The sparrow's gaze parallel to mine.
The eagle, high above, mocks me,
My dreams, weaker than the clouds.

Rising from the final illusion,
I stand as another self,
I stand as a man,
I shout loudly,
The far mountains are covered in snow,
Falling quietly.

The small cabin has become a fossil of memory,
The fallen bird calls and flying shadows
Still circle in my life,
Like a cello,
Melancholic, piercing through time and space.

三　預言　迷離洞簫

奔跑的梅花鹿和閃電的火狐
最終渴死在現代的井邊
端坐歲月的補丁之上
我還是喜歡被人喚作
山裡的漢子

一道又一道封鎖
一道又一道阻遏
我竭力穿越了城市之門
胸口突然長出的黑痣
暗示我城裡的道路很寬
但不能用來奔跑

不能用燈光取暖
不能在霓虹中晾曬靈魂
懷抱胸膛的烈火
我穿行在冰冷的預言裡
洞透預言的鷹　已死去多年

預言裡的世界　看盡黑夜的
不一定是最後的燈盞
花朵的背叛
有時和雪一樣潔白

III. Prophecy - Enigmatic Dizi

The running deer and lightning fox
Ultimately thirst to death at the modern well,
Sitting atop the patchwork of time,
I still prefer to be called
The man of the mountains.

A series of barricades,
A series of obstructions,
I struggle to pass through the city gates,
A black mole suddenly appearing on my chest,
Indicating that the roads in the city are wide,
But not for running.

No warmth from the light,
No soul drying in neon,
Embracing the fire in my chest,
I walk through the cold prophecy,
The eagle that pierced through prophecy
Has been dead for many years.

In the world of prophecy,
What sees the end of the night
Is not necessarily the final lamp.
The betrayal of flowers
Sometimes as pure as snow.

四　主題　性感薩克斯

從不記取城市的道路
地獄之上　天堂之下
每走一步　都是一次劫後餘生
指引我們最後魂歸的
不過是一隻神秘的烏鴉
所以我同時擁有兩種身份
白晝是遠古時代鳥的化石
黑夜是未來時空會飛的魚
我堅持只用堅硬的鬍鬚
試探人情冷暖

冷酷時　我體內有雪融
豪放時　我的靈覺馭山而飛
燦爛時　我攤開手掌
綻放命運錯過的花期
純淨時　我血管裡流著
藍色的血

或許我只需要一座房子
來忘記對墳墓的恐懼
一把椅子　將體重培育成刀子
又或者一個女人　用盡一生光陰
澆灌我開不了花的文字

IV. Theme - Sensual Saxophone

I never remember the roads of the city,
Above hell, below heaven,
Each step is a survival after disaster,
Guided by a mysterious crow,
So I possess two identities:
By day, a fossil of ancient birds,
By night, a fish that will fly in future time.
I insist on testing human warmth
With my hard whiskers.

In coldness, there is melting snow within me,
In boldness, my spirit rides the mountains and flies,
In brilliance, I spread my hands,
Letting the flowers of fate, missed in their bloom, unfold,
In purity, my veins carry
The blue blood of kings.

Perhaps all I need is a house
To forget my fear of graves,
A chair, to turn my weight into a knife,
Or perhaps a woman, who spends her entire life
Nurturing the words I cannot make bloom.

五　情節　欲斷管弦

作為歌手　我深知 C 調的高亢瞭亮
也深味生活的五線譜總是隨波逐流
懷抱聖樂　飲露的歌者
總是無處可棲
最後和宗教一起歸隱
我緣木求魚的歌聲曾經也很瞭亮
只是盡數落進了生活的痛處
我漸漸明白　歌聲
缺乏營養叫沙啞
飽食膏腴叫性感

我早已淡忘那些嘹亮的歲月
習慣並享受著物資攫取的快樂
我甚至忘了沒有比性感更致命的危險
失聲　也是創傷或者病變的惡果

V. Plot - Wanting to Cut the Strings

As a singer, I know well the sharpness of C major,
And taste how life's score always drifts with the waves,
Embracing sacred music,
The singer who drinks dew
Always finds no place to rest.
Finally, with religion, returns to hiding.
My once bright and clear voice,
Now falls into the pain of life,
I gradually understand—
A song that lacks nourishment is hoarse,
One that's well-fed is sensual.

I have long forgotten those clear years,
Accustomed to and enjoying the pleasures of material capture,
I even forgot that there is no greater danger than sensuality,
To lose my voice,
Is also a consequence of injury or illness.

六　旁白　無力小號

三十六年是多長一根鐵軌
失卻無數枕木的溫熱後
如果不能矗立成天梯
怎麼說　是生命
就會有一次絕唱

我更願意在依然抵達的驛站
把自己深深釘入某個黑夜
放棄所有憧憬和理想　一生安然
做帶病而唱的民間歌手

我相信
帶病　才能更深入疾苦
帶病　才能有更敏銳的觸覺感知疼痛
帶病　才能從容地將每一次登臺
都當作生命最後的演出
帶病　才能從死神的笑容
煉出生命的香

而我　註定要死在自己心裡
我的歌聲裡沒有悽惶

VI. Narration - Powerless Trumpet

Thirty-six years—how long a piece of iron track,
After losing countless warm ties,
If I cannot stand as a ladder to the heavens,
How can I call it life
Without an ultimate song?

I prefer, still arriving at the station,
To deeply nail myself into a certain black night,
Giving up all hopes and ideals, living peacefully,
Becoming a folk singer who sings while sick.

I believe—
Being sick allows one to delve deeper into suffering,
Being sick sharpens one's sensitivity to pain,
Being sick makes every performance feel like
The last show of life,
Being sick allows one to extract the fragrance of life
From the smile of death.

And I am destined to die within myself,
My song carries no sorrow.

風水與本命

一

重門　無字照壁　多叉的道口
臺灣二號　馬蹄蓮　花木密植
風水無邊　一頭嗆死在
這絕妙的佈局　鬼魅和人
相互錯身擦肩　陌路安詳
相根碩大且鋒利
骨頭飽蘸熱血的男人
流放於此　並犯下重煞

二

空心木隔牆的另一間辦公室
女人正在沒收室主的陽具
鬧出的動靜　讓隔壁的男人
付出一根肋骨皸裂的代價
償還被迫聽牆根的罪孽
倒地的一刻　他的身上揣著
老君山二當家法賜的太歲符

Feng Shui and Destiny

I

Heavy doors, a blank mirror wall, countless forked paths,
Taiwan No. 2, water lilies, dense planting of flowers and trees—
Boundless feng shui,
One head chokes to death in
This exquisite layout,
Ghosts and humans
Brush past each other,
Strangers walking the same peaceful path,
Roots large and sharp,
Men with bones soaked in hot blood,
Exiled here and committing great maleficence.

II

The hollow wood wall separating the office next door,
A woman is confiscating the landlord's genitals.
The noise causes the man in the next room
To pay with a cracked rib.
He pays for the sin of being forced to listen
To the sound from the corner of the wall.
In the moment he falls,
He carries the talisman of Tai Sui granted by the second in
command of Lao Jun Mountain.

三

老闆椅背後的牆上　不宜掛字
換了覆雪深沉的山水畫
埋在椅子裡的人從此失了體溫
金屬重甲包裹的窗戶外　一些鳥
來來去去　掉光了羽毛
保險櫃裡溢出的金水
彌散發餿的荷爾蒙氣息
只有智慧的烏鴉　遠遠地
發出刺耳的警告

四

矮個子猴兒占山為王
高個子猴兒謀取軍師
一群猢猻拱衛著母系的秩序
手持度牒的狗　懷抱狼的理想
悲劇不在於一根骨頭
破壞了物種秩序以及陰陽平衡
而是一枚無人認領的供果
暴露出深淵的線索

III

Behind the boss's chair,
It's bad feng shui to hang words,
Instead, a snow-covered, deep mountain and river painting
Replaces it.
The person sitting in the chair loses their body warmth,
Outside, the metal-armored window
Frames a few birds coming and going,
Dropping their feathers.
The golden liquid leaking from the safe
Spreads the rancid scent of hormones.
Only the wise crow, from afar,
Issues a sharp warning.

IV

The short monkey claims the mountain as king,
The tall monkey seeks to be the strategist.
A group of monkeys guards the matriarchal order,
Holding a dog's registration,
Embracing a wolf's ideals.
The tragedy isn't that a single bone
Disrupts the order of species and the balance of yin and yang,
But that an unclaimed offering fruit
Exposes the clues of the abyss.

五

四十二米的低空　適合
眺望人世已然模糊的過往
給上天的意志　挪出一絲清淨
枯坐陽臺的我　從不敢入定
怕丟了魂兒的肉身　輕慢
厄運和苦難　福賜的本命
其實　我一直感恩和敬畏著
昂首　只為等那一聲熟悉的鷹鳴
穿越白首　指引我
落日的家園

V

At 42 meters above the ground,
It's the perfect height to
View the blurry past of the human world.
Make way for a bit of purity
In the will of heaven.
Sitting still on the balcony, I never dare to settle,
Afraid of losing my soul's body,
Taking things lightly,
The misfortunes and hardships,
The blessings of destiny,
In truth, I have always been grateful and in awe of them,
Looking up only to await that familiar eagle's cry,
Piercing through old age, guiding me
To the home of the setting sun.

柬埔寨,那些醒著或痛著的時光

一　金邊　傷口裡的燈火

當金屬大鳥密閉的身體漸次透明
異鄉的燈火也亮了起來
把陌生國度粗礪的輪廓
勾勒成行者心中家的模樣

我不是行者　是逃難的人
從一場華麗無形的戰爭逃逸
我身體裡看不見的傷
需要一些　來自民間
沒有裝填風情的燈火療傷

而這飽經戰患的民間
從結痂的傷口捧出的燈火
照亮另一種傷口
喋血且新鮮

Cambodia: Those Awake or in Painful Times

I. Phnom Penh: The Lights in the Wounds

When the metallic birds of the sky gradually become transparent,
The lights of the foreign land also flicker on,
Outlining the rough contours of this unfamiliar country,
Turning it into a picture of home within the heart of a traveler.

I am not a traveler; I am a refugee,
Escaping from a grand, invisible war,
The wounds within my body unseen,
Needing the lights from the common folk,
Lights not filled with charm, but with healing power.

And this war-torn land,
From the scabbed-over wounds, the lights are held up,
Illuminating yet another wound—
Bleeding and fresh.

二　皇宮華麗的廢墟

在他們滿面的塵垢中
悲哀是一個多麼輕浮的詞根
眇目裡的人世到底還有沒有白晝
在他們支離破碎的身體上
生命是一個多麼輕浮的詞根
一隻胳膊　一條腿
命若遊絲地行走

是一群出沒戰爭的鬼
奪去他們人的形骸
從人世半掩的門伸出
乞討的手　一不小心
就拽出整個黑暗的地獄

II. The Palace's Splendid Ruins

In their faces covered with dust,
Sadness becomes such a fleeting root,
In their eyes, does the world still hold daylight?
On their broken bodies,
Life seems like such a light, meaningless root.
A single arm, a lone leg,
Moving like a thread of life, barely hanging on.

They are ghosts,
Plucked by war,
Taking away their human forms,
Their hands stretching out from the half-open door of the human world,
Unintentionally pulling forth the entire abyss of hell.

三　小木船　打撈的幸福

傾聽了太多的槍炮聲　以及
驚恐的呼號　慘烈的吶喊
還在以淚洗面的湄公河
早生的白髮披散了兩岸
那些屈死無辜的亡魂
繾綣在這人間最後的溫曖裡
茹毛飲血

戰爭可以奪去青春的留白
卻無法改變母性的堅貞
每次都是洶湧的初潮呵
肥了的魚兒都是她身體裡的卵

從她身體裡劃出的小木船
打撈一家三口的生活
是她懷裡死而復生的春夢
引誘陌生過客　陷身於
對某種虛擬幸福真實的構想

我分明看見自己水中的倒影
發出痙攣　無可言說的美妙

III. The Small Boat: Salvaging Happiness

Having heard too much of the guns,
The frightened screams, and the harsh cries,
Still on the Mekong, which weeps with tears,
The early gray hair cascades along the banks,
Those innocent souls, dying unjustly,
Lingering in the final warmth of this world,
Living on raw flesh and blood.

War can steal the innocence of youth,
But cannot change a mother's steadfastness.
Every time, it is the surging first tide,
The fish fattened, carrying the eggs of her body.

The small boat she carves from herself,
Salvages the life of a family of three,
It is the spring dream that dies and is reborn in her embrace,
Luring strangers into sinking
Into the false reality of happiness.

I clearly see my reflection in the water,
Spasming, an indescribable beauty.

四　暹粒河　雨季的恩澤

純潔　因為源自那些石頭的靈魂
香火浴身的佛主懷抱一個王朝
坐在你絲絲縷縷編織的柔情裡
沒有一絲邪念

我甚至相信　在光陰逝去以前
在雨季沒有抵達暹粒河以前
在愛恨沒有遭遇時空以前
這些鏤刻了樸素祈願的石頭
曾經和雨一樣柔軟

暹粒河　如果是造物主的旨意
請忘記你的愛憎吧讓　這一場季雨
訴盡下個輪回的悲憫
讓一個虔誠的民族　從深創的胸膛
捧出一個嶄新的魚米之鄉

記住那些石頭銘記的一切吧
這塵世　只有柔軟的內心
可以抵禦一切苦難
冷硬地窺視

IV. Siem Reap River: Blessings of the Rainy Season

Purity, For it comes from the souls of stones,
In the embrace of the Buddha, who bathes in incense,
a dynasty is born,
Sitting in the tender emotions you have woven,
With no trace of evil thoughts.

I even believe, before time passes,
Before the rainy season reaches Siem Reap River,
Before love and hate encounter time and space,
These stones, engraved with simple prayers,
Once were soft like rain.

Siem Reap River, if this is the will of the Creator,
Please forget your love and hate,
Let this seasonal rain
Narrate the pity of the next cycle,
And allow a devout nation, from the deep wound in its chest,
To bring forth a brand new land of fish and rice.

Remember all that these stones inscribe,
For in this world, only a soft heart
Can withstand all suffering,
Coldly peering from afar.

五　毗濕奴　神圖騰的純度

毗濕奴
如果只是關於男人的命題
凝固的火無法燃燒
你還能這麼堅挺地矗立於世麼

毗濕奴
日輪　蓮花　海螺與劍
你暗示在法器的寓意
生生不滅的火
其實源于水的子宮

磕頭　叩拜　敬香　祈禱
走出水火的男人和女人們
蜂擁闖入金石壘築的幻夢

渾忘了所有立世的輝煌
都只是建立在一種純粹的圖騰之上
毗濕奴　儘管你挺拔如昔
我卻看見你枯萎的內心
一如這戰火中皸裂貧瘠的土地

V. Vishnu: The Purity of the Divine Totem

Vishnu,
If you are only about man's fate,
The frozen fire cannot burn,
Can you still stand so tall in this world?

Vishnu,
The sun, the lotus, the conch, and the sword,
You hint at the meaning of the sacred instruments,
That eternal fire,
Actually originates from the womb of water.

Bowing, praying, offering incense,
Men and women, emerging from fire and water,
Rush into the illusory dream built of stone and gold.

Forgetting that all earthly glory
Is built upon a pure totem,
Vishnu, though you remain upright as ever,
I see the withered heart inside you,
Just like this land cracked and barren from the fires of war.

六　巴芳寺　歷史的遺裳

在光陰裡坐得太久　雕像已流不出汗來
平民的守望已經荒煙蔓草
逝去皇朝威嚴的氣象
還被石獅們含在滾燙的嘴裡

這來來往往本是佛的足印
誰以信徒的名義　驅趕人性
獲取殺戮中的快感　當石頭的預言
被一千年後的熱血證實
森嚴的皇官　你只是穿在
死去歷史身上華貴的遺裳

為你而生而死的人
在民間開始新的輪回
而那些高懸於廟堂的鏡框
搖搖欲墜於似我這般
布衣草民地逼視

VI. Baphuon Temple: The Garb of History

Having sat too long in time, the statues can no longer sweat,
The vigilance of the common people is now overtaken by weeds,
The imposing aura of the fallen dynasty,
Still held in the hot mouths of stone lions.

The footprints of the Buddha once walked here,
Who in the name of faith,
Drove away humanity,
To gain pleasure from murder?
When the stone's prophecy
Was proven by the blood of a thousand years,
The stern imperial officers, you are just wearing
The lavish garb of a dead history.

Those born and died for you,
Now begin a new cycle in the common folk,
While the framed mirrors hanging in the temples
Sway and almost fall,
As if to be scrutinized by commoners like me.

七　吳哥　觸摸的幻覺

眾神引退　廢墟遼闊
我屏息躡足而行　生恐
一場千年繁華猝然坍塌在凝固的夢裡

從骨子裡沁出的汗水與頭頂的烈日無關
一如這殘垣斷壁與膚淺的時光無關
從自己的君王走成創世傳說的信徒
脫水的肉身更適合接受信仰的沐浴

我濡濕的靈魂穿越道道城門　四處遊走
石壁上眾神復活　神情肅穆
聖火繚繞的祭臺上
神話永久催眠了真相

洶湧的紅塵在凝固的史詩中倉皇倒退
巴芳寺無處不在的永恆微笑
讓我的手在冷硬的石壁上
竟然摸到了人間的溫度

踉踉蹌蹌跌倒在幻覺深處
返回　就成為今生最大的恐懼

VII. Angkor: The Illusion of Touch

The gods retreat, the ruins are vast,
I hold my breath and tread carefully,
Fearing that a thousand years of glory will suddenly collapse in the frozen dream.

The sweat seeping from my bones has nothing to do with the scorching sun,
Just as these crumbled walls have nothing to do with superficial time.
From my own king to the followers of the creation myth,
My desiccated body is more suited to receiving the baptism of faith.

My soaked soul passes through the gates, wandering,
On the stone walls, the gods revive, their expressions solemn,
On the altar where the holy fire lingers,
Myths forever hypnotize the truth.

The surging world in the frozen epic retreats in a panic,
Baphuon Temple's ever-present eternal smile,
Causes my hand to touch the warmth of the world
On the cold, hard stone walls.

Stumbling, I fall deep into the illusion,
And returning becomes my greatest fear.

硯梅有香

這人世　總有一些無以隱忍的大淨
牽引我們回到生命最初的寧謐
譬如母親薄如枯葉的身影
譬如父親就快凝固的笑容
譬如嬰兒的眼淚
譬如大洋彼岸
不落朱砂的小腳印

隨一朵飄墜的雪花或是落梅
爺爺奶奶無數次踏穿夢境
以雪花之輕　落梅之香
為你題寫的人生封面
再肆虐的病毒又如何抵達
這人間最深沉的隱喻

初生嬰兒的小腳丫　一如雪花
這穿越時空　白色的火焰
可以高蹈於所有苦難的深淵

抑或飛越人世最神聖的福祉
在抵達爺爺奶奶懷抱之前
黑白分明有梅香指引的世界
才不會迷路

Ink Plum Fragrance

In this world,
there are always some unbearable moments of great purity,
pulling us back to the tranquility of life's beginnings—
like the figure of my mother, thin as dried leaves,
like my father's smile, soon to freeze,
like the tears of a newborn,
like the footprints of small feet
left on the other side of the ocean,
where no vermilion ink has ever touched.

With a falling snowflake or a plum blossom,
grandparents have walked through my dreams countless times.
With the lightness of snow, the fragrance of plums,
they wrote the cover of your life.
No matter how savage the viruses may be,
how could they reach
the deepest metaphor of this world?

The tiny footprints of a newborn, like snowflakes—
this white flame that crosses time and space,
can dance above the deepest abyss of suffering.

Or perhaps, it soars past the world's most sacred blessings,
before reaching the embrace of my grandparents,
a world, clear in black and white,
with the fragrance of plums to guide the way.
It will not lose its path.

在硯梅涸潤的紙上
落一場快意的水墨雪
在我們被徹底淨化的意念深處
聽　落梅以另一種形式盛開
聽　雪花以精靈的名義訴說
聽　光陰滴落成淚
聽　人生至柔的深情

On ink-soaked paper, the fragrance of plums,
falling like a joyful snowstorm,
in the depths of our purified thoughts,
listen: the plums bloom in another form,
listen: the snow speaks, in the name of spirits,
listen: time drips into tears,
listen: the deepest love of life, soft and tender.

五隻羊

——兼致王小忠

小忠用宅急送的方式
寄來兩千公里外　甘南草原的
《五隻羊》和青稞酒
我欣然准允鎖在窗外的陽光
進駐我的鋼筋城堡

在牧人的心裡　草原
是向天借來易碎的鏡子
鏡中所有生命的成像
都必須保持雲朵一樣的輕靈

牛羊蹈火的蹄聲很輕
風誦讀的經幡很輕
透過燈花兒　忘了時間
老阿媽的眺望也很輕

只在繁星密織的夜晚
那些白日裡遙不可及
我們膜拜和仰望的福祉

以煙火的姿態回到人間
回到草場　回到氈房
回到牛羊尋覓低處的
根和愛

Five Sheep
— *To Wang Xiaozhong*

Xiaozhong sent it by express delivery,
two thousand kilometers away from Gannan Grassland,
Five Sheep and green raw liquor.
I gladly allowed the sunlight locked outside my window
to settle into my concrete fortress.

In the heart of the herder, the grassland
is a fragile mirror borrowed from the sky,
reflecting all the life within it,
where every image must remain as light as the clouds.

The sound of hooves, light as they step through fire,
the wind reciting the prayer flags, light as they flutter,
through the light of the lamp's bloom, forgetting time,
even the old grandmother's gaze is light.

Only at night, under the thick weave of stars,
those blessings we worship and gaze upon during the day,
become within reach.

In the form of fireworks, it returns to the world,
back to the pasture, back to the felt house,
back to the cattle and sheep, seeking the low places,
their roots and love.

草場一天比一天瘦
羊群一天比一天零落
五隻羊來不及整理離群的孤獨
主人的命運軌跡已然輪回於
背棄了使命的月光裡
草原寂靜鐘聲寂靜
所有生命寂靜
如一紙經文
落地為安

而我在遙遠他鄉
與一壺青稞酒寂靜的對話
足以讓血管中燃起熾烈的火焰
無聲　卻無所不達

The pasture grows thinner with each passing day,
the sheep more scattered by the hour.
Five sheep, too late to arrange their loneliness after leaving the flock,
the fate of the herder already revolved
in the moonlight that abandoned its mission.
The grassland is silent, the bells silent,
all life is silent,
like a scripture,
falling to rest.

And I, in a faraway land,
speak silently with a pot of raw liquor,
enough to set a fierce fire burning in my veins—
silent, yet reaching everywhere.

在冬天寫一些關於春天的詩句

一

任性的春天
還一直逗留在枝頭的桃紅柳綠
無邊的春色卻早已在人間
氾濫成勾魂攝魄的一片白

二

家裡的一盆君子蘭
持續盛放了好幾個年頭
讓我心懷感恩並羞愧著
這些年面對逆境和厄運
我一次也沒盛開過
於是我決定
把自己也種進土裡

Writing Some Spring Poems in Winter

I

The willful spring
lingers still on peach blossoms and willow greens.
Endless spring colors, yet in the world,
flood into a soul-stirring sea of white.

II

A pot of Clivia at home,
continues to bloom year after year.
I am both grateful and ashamed—
in the face of adversity and misfortune,
I have never bloomed once.
So I've decided
to plant myself in the soil.

三

校園裡
飛馳的英俊單車小少年
啪的一聲尖銳
在地上畫出漂亮的圓弧
脫口而出的"完美"
讓迎面走來的美少女
張大的嘴比摔裂的手機
開口更大
心裡微痛漾開
目光卻淨拾一段人間大美

四

繁花擠痛眼睛的時節
我們渾忘了叫做草的植物
但一定不能忘記　蚍蜉
並不是春天的唯一隱私
米粒兒一般　幾隻迷路的小蚍蜉
致命地爬进了乘機旅客的手機裡
一段驚悚的視頻讓候機樓
搖晃得厲害
我用剛下達佈局藥殺的手
轉身寫下如是貌似詩歌的文字
這個和蚍蜉一起擁有的春天
我和詩歌被賦予無窮生命力

III

On campus,
a young boy rides his bicycle with grace,
with a sharp "snap"
he draws a beautiful arc on the ground.
The word "perfect" escapes his lips,
making the beautiful girl walking towards him
open her mouth wider than the cracked phone.
A slight ache spreads in my heart,
but my gaze captures a great beauty in this world.

IV

In the season when the blooming flowers strain our eyes,
we forget the plants called grass,
but we must never forget that cockroaches
are not the only secrets of spring.
Tiny, like grains of rice,
a few lost cockroaches crawl
deadly into the smartphones of passengers.
A terrifying video shakes the terminal,
and with my hand freshly delivering poison,
I turn to write what seems like poetry.
In this spring, shared with cockroaches,
I and poetry are endowed with endless vitality.

五

提著燈盞趕路　山裡的孩子
用了四十多年　一寸寸回收
不再驚濤駭浪的影子
燈盞回到肩頭的時候
他丟失了最後一座山頭
從此改走水路

他的另一隻肩頭上
趴著的小天使
在上面打嗝　打盹兒　吐奶　吐泡泡
並以此定義所有溢滿奶香的日子
是一個中年男人無以饒恕的罪孽

V

The child in the mountains, carrying a lantern,
has spent over forty years, inch by inch,
reclaiming shadows that no longer roar.
When the lantern reaches his shoulder,
he has lost the last mountain peak,
and from then on, he takes to the water.

On the other shoulder,
a little angel lies,
burping, napping, spitting milk, blowing bubbles,
defining all the days full of milk fragrance
as a sin that an aging man cannot forgive.

六

老易　今天怎麼還不給我報班
此際　焦頭爛額的老易
正突圍在滿地金屬的重圍中
時針著急指向八點五十

電話裡的稚嫩童聲來自
上學路上的四歲小布丁
我分明聽見　潛伏在側
妻子臉上淌著
奶一樣潔白的笑

必須承認
這是讓人骨酥筋軟的甜蜜導演
我剛想把右腳放在油門上
卻被劈頭蓋臉的紅燈
瞪了個趔趄

想想搖籃裡
還在奶水裡磨牙的小卿安
我本能地挺直了脊背
從此再無法預謀的餘生
與三個女人的短兵相接
誰來指教

VI

Old Yi, why haven't you reported my class yet?
At this moment, the troubled Old Yi
is breaking through the siege of scattered metals.
The hour hand hurriedly points to 8:50.

The childish voice on the phone
comes from a four-year-old pudding on the way to school.
I clearly hear the sound of
the wife's milk-like smile slipping down her face.

I must admit,
this is the sweet director who makes one's bones turn soft.
Just as I think to put my right foot on the gas,
a red light stuns me with a jolt.

Thinking of little Qing'an,
still gnawing on the milk in her crib,
I instinctively straighten my back.
From then on, there is no way to prearrange the rest of my life
as I clash with three women in a daily struggle.
Who will offer advice?

七

飯後一支煙
快速治癒厭食的焦慮
煙頭欲飛
黑色大口罩　紅色反光背心
以及揮舞的鐵掃帚
眼前的她們是我的員工

我卻叫不出名字
攥緊了煙頭
從她們身邊經過的一瞬
我在想　一個禮拜
都在吃著泡菜炒肉末的她們
會不會和我一樣
也患上了厭食症

VII

A cigarette after dinner
quickly soothes the anxiety of anorexia.
The cigarette butt about to fly,
a black face mask, a red reflective vest,
and a sweeping iron broom,
the women in front of me are my employees.

Yet, I can't remember their names.
Tightening my grip on the cigarette,
as I pass by them,
I wonder if, after a week of eating kimchi stir-fried meat,
they too suffer from anorexia, like me.

八

電梯裡
她一個勁兒地往裡擠
我拼了命地向後靠
直到把自己貼在電梯壁上
始終沒敢出一口氣

出了電梯
她笑著問我
怎麼瘦得像張照片
我瞬間憂慮自己
還是不是彩色的

九

淺灰衛衣　深藍板鞋　微卷的長髮
黑色斜跨肩包　手機　香煙和滑板
似一縷不羈自由的雲影
飄過校園搖曳的紅櫻大道
飄過我的眼前　作為父親
我目光裡生出的疼痛
硌傷好長一段光陰

VIII

In the elevator,
she relentlessly squeezes in.
I lean back, desperately,
until I am pressed against the elevator wall,
not daring to breathe.

When we exit the elevator,
she smiles and asks,
"Why are you so thin, like a photo?"
I instantly worry about whether
I'm still in color.

IX

A light gray sweatshirt, dark blue sneakers, slightly curled long hair,
a black crossbody bag, phone, cigarette, and skateboard—
she floats by, a free cloud,
over the red cherry avenue of the campus.
She passes before my eyes, and as a father,
the pain that emerges in my gaze
grinds deep for a long time.

十

皮膚粗糲　衣著邋遢
軍膠和蛇皮袋
被時代換做農民工的他
此刻佇立在開滿櫻花的路旁

有人經過
慌忙佯裝看手機
沒人的時候
高舉了手機對著櫻花

其實　櫻花爛漫
開得不帶一絲偏見

十一

十萬伏的高壓電線上
長滿了密密麻麻的黑色小血栓

隔著冷漠的窗玻
我在腦子裡
密謀殺戮的念頭
突然眼前一黑
電線上那些爪握十萬伏兵的小精靈
還給我致命一擊

X

Rough skin, untidy clothes,
military rubber boots and a snake-skin bag—
he, transformed by the era into a migrant worker,
now stands by the road, lined with cherry blossoms.

When someone passes,
they hastily pretend to look at their phone.
When no one is around,
he raises his phone, aiming it at the cherry blossoms.

But actually, the cherry blossoms bloom,
unbiased and unprejudiced.

XI

On the high-voltage line of 100,000 volts,
thick black blood clots grow.

Through the indifferent window glass,
I plot thoughts of murder in my mind.
Suddenly, everything goes black,
and those little sprites clutching 100,000 volts on the wires
deal me a fatal blow.

落葉不哭

一

落葉不哭　大地懷抱正暖
接納淬火的生命

寂寞的盡頭　不是天堂
童話的故鄉　有綠色的牧笛　聲聲召喚

從故鄉到異鄉　從異鄉到天堂
誰不是一直在路上

路上　靈魂有淚　命運是河
惟大地內心的悲喜不露半點聲色

告別酒香的靈魂　獨自上路
以青鳥的翔姿棲居燦爛星河

落葉不哭　乘哪一陣風
不是陽光下的漂泊

The Falling Leaves Do Not Cry

I

The falling leaves do not cry, for the earth's embrace is warm,
accepting life tempered by fire.

At the end of loneliness, there is no paradise.
In the homeland of fairy tales,
a green shepherd's flute calls, time and again.

From homeland to foreign land, from foreign land to paradise,
who is not always on the road?

On the road, the soul sheds tears, fate is a river,
but the earth's heart reveals no sign of sorrow or joy.

Bidding farewell to the soul's scent of wine, I travel alone,
like a blue bird, soaring to rest in the splendid galaxy.

The falling leaves do not cry, carried by whichever wind,
not drifting under the sun.

二

我們都已經在路上
只是遭遇了不同的風景
暫時的駐腳　抑或永久的停息
只能證明我們成了風景的一部分

你都看見了什麼　天使舞在風景裡
迷路的魔鬼　瘋狂尋找自己的影子

你看見別人時　自己現形的一半
鏤刻在白晝還是黑夜

目光銹蝕的永遠不會是真相
逝風吹散的　不是露

而露光折射的風景
是我們永遠無法抵達的真相

II

We are all already on the road,
only encountering different landscapes.
A temporary stop, or a permanent rest,
only proves we have become part of the landscape.

What did you see? Angels dance in the scenery,
lost devils frantically search for their own shadows.

When you see others,you see half of your own reflection,
etched in either daylight or night.

Eyes rusted with time will never reveal the truth.
The wind that scatters the passing days is not the dew,

but the scenery refracted by the dew's light,
is a truth we will never reach.

三

有人在大嚼文字的盛宴後悄然退場
說　想找個沒有饑荒的地方

人間的風花　一直在磨損陽光的質地
端著酒杯　我始終找不到潮濕的原因

溺水三千　作一回牛飲的漢子吧
哪怕最終以葬身　為紅顏命名

可七月的風　總是輕浮地說三道四
撩拔神經脆弱的門窗
一扇窗打開　驚呼魔鬼的拜訪
一扇門打開　喜迎天使的降臨

半生徘徊在虛構邊緣的人
以提前的遠行　換取靈魂的永寧

塵世的嘴很燙　路上的魂兒卻冷了
在這個酷熱的夏季　陽光也在蒙難

讓我的身影落地長成一棵樹吧
我想聽聽　落葉會怎樣哭泣

III

Someone quietly exits after feasting on words,
saying, "I want to find a place with no famine."

The winds and flowers of the world continue to wear away the quality of sunlight,
holding a wine glass, but I can never find the reason for dampness.
Drown in the three thousand rivers, be the man who drinks like a beast,
even if in the end, I die, named in honor of beauty.

But the July winds always speak too lightly,
stirring the fragile nerves of doors and windows.
One window opens, shouting with the devil's visit,
another opens, welcoming the angel's arrival.

A person wandering at the edge of fiction,
trades an early journey for the eternal peace of the soul.

The world's mouth is scorching, yet the soul on the road is cold,
in this scorching summer, even the sunlight suffers.

Let my shadow fall and grow into a tree,
I want to hear how the falling leaves will cry.

清明人間

這雨　在古詩裡下了一千多年
而在更加浩渺的時空裡
她們是趕路的花朵
帶著潔白的使命

憂傷如風　撫遍逝者福祉
以及生者的每一寸山河
至美時刻的黯然神傷
一直是人類無法治癒的病
而這一次懷念疼痛的箭矢
擊中準確的目標
也擊中一個詩人
預謀的傷情

又何止清明　無時無刻
每一個來的人　去的人
不是被死神包圍
就是與死神同行
最終死路一條的人世
再沒有比死更值得認真的事

我不願去記憶臨界的地址
那個認真活了一輩子的老頭兒
把最後的笑容遺落成生命密碼
被一些白色或黃色的花朵破譯

The Clear Tomb of Humanity

This rain,
has been falling in ancient poems for over a thousand years,
and in even vaster realms of time,
it is the flowers on their journey,
carrying a pure and sacred mission.

Sadness, like the wind, touches
the blessings of the departed
and every inch of the living's mountains and rivers.
The sorrow at the most beautiful moments,
has always been a disease humanity cannot heal.
And this time, the arrow of nostalgic pain
strikes the target with precision,
hitting a poet's premeditated wound.

It is not just Qingming, but every moment,
every person who comes, and every person who goes,
either surrounded by death,
or walking alongside it.
In the end, the road to death is the only way forward—
nothing in this life deserves more attention than death itself.

I do not wish to remember the address of the edge,
that old man who lived earnestly his entire life,
left his final smile as a life's password,
which was deciphered by some white or yellow flowers.

而我一步一步行走的這個清明
仿若五十年前來的時候

雨和花朵行走的時節
我們不妨隱身　留一條道路
給塵世以遠　生命以遠

And this Qingming, step by step,
is like the one I came to fifty years ago.

When rain and flowers walk together,
perhaps we should hide ourselves,
leaving a road open—
for the dust of the world, and for life, to journey far.

狼 道

一

對著日頭打盹兒的牧童
頭枕著狼來了的寓言
狼來了　沒有披著羊皮
狼走了　羊皮攥在獵人手上

此刻　一隻手和一隻爪
相向　遭遇　對抗　交融
一隻沉睡的狼　從我內心醒來

不像人類　慣於巧舌如簧
我們只仰首嘯月
感恩長生天的恩賜
噬盡最後一口獵物
是對生命最莊重的葬禮

相較于人世蟄伏　狼深知
唯有比雪輕　比草韌的爪
才能捕捉稍縱即逝的戰機
一爪致命　一擊功成

此刻　我以狼爪為筆
寫下關於狼的文字
字裡行間的血腥與殺氣
是你們未敢涉足的狼性天道

The Wolf's Way

I

A shepherd boy dozes against the sun
His head pillowed on the fable of The Wolf Is Coming
The wolf comes, no sheepskin slung over its back
The wolf leaves, the sheepskin clenched in the hunter's hand

Now, a hand and a claw
Face each other, meet, clash, merge
A sleeping wolf wakes within my soul

Unlike humans, masters of glib tongues
We only tilt our heads and howl at the moon
Grateful for the grace of the Eternal Sky
To devour the last bite of prey
Is the most solemn funeral for life

Compared to lying low in the mortal world, the wolf knows well
Only a claw, lighter than snow, tougher than grass
Can seize the fleeting chance of battle
One claw to strike fatally, one blow to claim success

Now, I take a wolf's claw as my pen
To write words of the wolf
The blood and menace between the lines
Are the wolf's innate way of heaven, where you dare not step

二

荒原　曠野　幽谷　險灘
不屑人類童話的狼群
隱匿或出沒　直面生存
一隻狼是一柄孤刃
一群狼　是一片呼嘯的鋒

為生存奔襲　以奔襲生存
狼以颶風之勢突圍宿命佈局
沒有羊　草原沒有脈動
沒有狼　草原已然死去

羊吃草　狼吃羊的時候
閉著眼睛的草原沒有淚水
傾聽的牧草卻長出了骨頭
大地用一隻乳房餵羊
另一隻乳房餵狼

回到最初　抑或最後的領地
狼的世界　從無兒戲
拿捏文字的人類　一支筆
書寫狼性光輝激蕩的文明史
一支筆招魂農耕哲學的遺響

狼齒噬淨的人去了天堂
槍聲洗淨的狼亦歸彼蒼
天堂路上　人性與狼性之間
唯風過牧草　簌簌低回

II

Wasteland, wilderness, deep valley, dangerous shoal
Wolf packs that scorn human fairy tales
Lurk or roam, facing survival head-on
A single wolf is a lone blade
A pack of wolves is a whistling blaze of sharpness

Rush for survival, survive by rushing
Wolves break through the weave of fate like a hurricane
Without sheep, the grassland has no pulse
Without wolves, the grassland is already dead

When sheep graze, and wolves devour sheep
The grassland, eyes closed, sheds no tears
Yet the listening grass blades grow bones
The earth feeds sheep with one breast
And wolves with the other

Back to the first, or the last, territory
There is no play in the wolf's world
Humans who wield words—with one pen
They write the stirring civilization history of wolfhood's glory
With another, they call back the fading echo of agrarian philosophy

Humans gnawed clean by wolf teeth go to heaven
Wolves cleansed by gunshots also return to the firmament
On the road to heaven, between humanity and wolfhood
Only the wind stirs the grass, rustling softly and low

最深刻的語言

父親走了
母親加速了衰老
終日慽慽
用毫無生氣的眼睛
看這日漸遠離的世界
和與她不再相關的日子

一生不善言辭的母親
開始尋找機會
和她的兒子深談
那些長滿青苔的久遠時光
以及與她身世有關的話題
所有的鋪墊
只為埋藏多年的秘密
外婆留下的嫁妝
是時候換個守護的人了

她說　父親走了
被日子過了一輩子
兩個人的生活　現在
才感覺每一個日子
都很重

The Deepest Language

Father has passed away,
and Mother's aging has accelerated.
She's sluggish all day,
watching the world drift further away with lifeless eyes,
and days that are no longer related to her.

Mother, who was never good with words,
begins to seek opportunities
to have deep conversations with her son,
about the long-ago times overgrown with moss
and the topics tied to her own life.
All the prelude
is to bury a long-kept secret.
The dowry left by Grandma
is now due for a new guardian.

She says, "Father is gone,
life has passed by him for a lifetime.
The life of two people—now,
we finally feel that each day
is so heavy."

在她心理一直引以為豪
會寫文章會作詩的兒子
一聲不吭　內心的潮湧
就快漫過眼眶
母親　這世間還有什麼
比安靜躺在墓地的老頭兒
凝固在墓碑上的笑
更深刻的語言

In her mind, she has always been proud
of her son, who could write articles and compose poetry.
But now, silent and with a swelling tide inside,
he is on the verge of tears.
Mother, in this world, is there anything
more profound than the old man,
quietly lying in the grave,
and his smile frozen on the gravestone?

油茶花

> 天空為鏡,許你以主角,掌三尺蒼生。
> ——題記

一

又或者打馬回到前世
那時候　柴門和雪
竹籬和月　拒絕
詩詞意境的冷
那時候　你芸薹的身世
遠在煙火之上

二

一次凝目
山河放牧著山河
一次屏息
春色深入了春色
一次冥想
時間開出金黃的秘
人世由此
歸於安詳

Canola Flowers

The sky is a mirror, granting you the role of protagonist, wielding three feet of the living world.
                                                        —*Inscription*

I

Or perhaps, riding back to a past life,
when the thatched gate and the snow
the bamboo fence and the moon, rejected
the coldness of poetic realms.
Back then, your life as a mustard plant
existed far beyond the realm of fireworks.

II

Once, a gaze fixed upon the world,
mountains and rivers grazing each other.
Once, a breath held,
spring's colors merging with more spring's hues.
Once, a meditation,
time blossomed into golden secrets,
and from this,
the world found peace.

三

梨花過早淪陷
枝頭寫意的困境
一塵不染的獻詞
讓玉蘭痛失了歸宿
而你　鹽一般樸素的哲學
讓塵埃有了高度

四

是一些帶著神諭
小小的使者
深入一種遼闊的理想
大地回到多情
蒼生得以蕩漾
這時候　任何讚美
都是偽善

五

以礁石的忠誠
面對你　面對
又一季春天
所有舉杯向天的虔敬
是關於生命福祉的隱喻

III

The pear blossoms fell too soon,
branches writing their own dilemma.
The untainted ode
caused the magnolia to lose its home.
And you, with a salt-like simplicity,
gave the dust height.

IV

There are those carrying oracles,
small messengers,
entering a vast and distant ideal.
The earth returns to its passion,
and the people are swayed.
At this moment, any praise
is hypocrisy.

V

With the loyalty of a reef,
I face you, face
another season of spring.
All the reverence of raising a cup to the sky
is an allegory of life's blessings.

六

如果罌粟的毒
並非源自華麗世襲
你且學那偷香的蝶
試一試　這死水微瀾的人間
溺死的渴望　魅惑如讖

七

命犯桃花的三月
我以此自贖
並構想關於生命
一場浩渺宏大的結局
便是任一粒油菜花的籽
從內心生長出發
直抵異次元的輪回

VI

If the poison of the poppy
did not arise from a glorious inheritance,
then learn, like the butterfly stealing fragrance,
to test the stagnant waters of this world,
where drowned desires,
mesmerizing like prophecies, beckon.

VII

In the peach blossom-filled March,
I redeem myself through this,
and envision a vast and grand conclusion to life.
It is that any seed of canola flowers,
growing from the heart,
would reach the reincarnation of another dimension.

三疊人間

一

卸了這一襲裹身的布衣
骷髏般決絕無畏地行走
只為證明所有活著的疼痛
從來無關華麗的世襲

眉骨以上　下頜以下
隱藏人鬼的界碑　可怕的
不是血光　輕易迸濺
是命運的鋒刃
懸而未落

蓄須以觸世
不肯輕易就戮
生存刺骨的真相
你們說的風塵布衣
是我提前轉世的靈魂

Three Layers of the Mortal World

I

Cast off this linen robe clinging to my frame
Walk with the resolute fearlessness of a skeleton
Only to prove that all the pain of living
Has never been tied to the splendor of hereditary fame

Above the brow bone, below the jaw
Lies the boundary stone between human and ghost.
What's terrifying
It is not the blood light, it is spattering easily
But the sharp blade of fate
Hanging, yet never falling

Grow a beard to touch the world
Refuse to be slain without a fight
The bone-chilling truth of survival
The dusty linen robe you speak of
Is my soul, reincarnated ahead of time

二

記取陽光的味道　落葉安詳
記取光陰的味道　我亦安詳
躺在光陰的水晶棺裡
細讀每一片落葉
劫後餘生的過往

穿自己衣服的石頭　乾淨
吃自己糧食的草木　乾淨
我亦乾淨　赤條條來去
餐風飲露後
歸還大地

曾經寫下的字字句句
是此生唯一
脫不掉的囚衣

II

Remember the taste of sunlight, the peace of fallen leaves
Remember the taste of time, and I too am at peace
Lying in a crystal coffin of time
I read every fallen leaf carefully
The past that survived the catastrophe

Stones wearing their own clothes are pure
Plants eating their own grain are pure
I too am pure, coming and going naked
After feasting on wind and dew
I return to the earth

Every word I once wrote
Is the only prison robe in this life
That can never be taken off

三

做你音樂春天的蝴蝶
做你藍調愛情的王子
做你靈魂漫野的雲
只無關天堂

一季花開　一場雪融
兩枚音符之間的輪回
一闋前世　迷離
一闋今生　明媚

你燦爛的音樂
原是極致宿命
死在聆聽之後的人
早已身中劇毒

靈魂是只怎樣的野獸
舔舐傷口方得自愈
恰似你的旋律　雅尼
在被下一枚音符
擊穿魂魄之前
你還我布衣
我還你肉身

III

Be a butterfly in the spring of your music
Be a prince in the blues of your love
Be a cloud wandering wild in your soul
Nothing to do with heaven, though

A season of blooming flowers, a melt of snow
Reincarnation between two musical notes
One verse of the past, blurred
One verse of the present, bright

Your brilliant music
Turns out to be the ultimate fate
Those who die after listening
Have long been fatally poisoned

What kind of beast is the soul?
It licks its wounds to heal itself
Just like your melody, Yanni
Before the next musical note
Pierces the soul
You return my linen robe to me
And I return your flesh to you

瀘山祭

一

最初的一粒火星
此刻　終於喊出
一棵樹的疼痛
十萬火焰　十萬棵樹
一起喊出的疼痛
叫做瀘山

二

當陽光成為隱喻
月光陷入虛擬
瀘山　你萬年的修行
沒禁得住一粒火苗的挑逗
蹈火的人　化身舍利
見證一個時代的良知

Lushan Rite

I

The first spark of fire,
At this moment, finally cries out,
The pain of a tree.
A hundred thousand flames, a hundred thousand trees,
Together they cry out in pain,
This is called Lushan.

II

When sunlight becomes a metaphor,
Moonlight sinks into the virtual,
Lushan, your millennia of cultivation
Couldn't withstand the temptation of a single spark.
The fire-walkers transform into relics,
Witnessing the conscience of an era.

三

火焰打開的深淵
灰燼寫成的遺囑
瓊海　每一朵
洗淨塵心的浪花
至此　斷了輪回
而西昌　這一次你丟失的
是塵世最美的袈裟

四

失血的花瓶
耗盡畫家手中最後一滴墨
紅色菊花
是火焰之上的梵音
此起披落間
遠去的人背著經書
回到火焰的內心

III

The abyss opened by the flames,
The will written in ashes,
Qiong Hai—every wave
Washes away the dust of the heart.
Thus, the cycle of reincarnation ends,
And Xichang, this time you lost
The most beautiful robe of the mundane world.

IV

The blood-drained vase,
Consumes the last drop of ink in the painter's hand.
Red chrysanthemums,
The sacred sound above the flames.
With every rise and fall,
The departed ones carry their scriptures,
Returning to the heart of the fire.

暗夜鏡像

一

無主夜貓　把牆根叫得搖搖晃晃
蟲鳴聚力　擊穿夜的厚黑
一牆之隔　沉默的耳朵
生生逼出我內心的冷芒

當沐浴如新的日頭如約而至
我將再次站在抉擇的隘口
以一枚金幣的名義
鍍苟且以閃耀證詞
或是還原水的姿態
給紫宸以致命一擊

二

把自己和被子疊成豆腐塊
搓洗比這季衣衫更薄的身體
貌似循規蹈矩的日子
原是一語道破的謎面

避開那些淬了冰的目光
口罩遮蓋我的另一張臉
一張肉體侘寂之後
偷渡另一時空的臉

Mirror of the Dark Night

I

Ownerless stray cats wail, shaking the wall's base to its core
Insects chirp in unison, piercing the night's thick blackness
On the other side of the wall, silent ears
Forge a cold glint from the depths of my soul

When the sun, washed clean as new, arrives as promised
I will stand again at the pass of choice
In the name of a gold coin
Plate mediocrity with a shining testimony
Or return to the form of water
Strike the Purple Palace with a fatal blow

II

Fold myself and the quilt into a tofu cube
Scrub a body thinner than the clothes of this season
These days that seem to follow the rules
Are but a riddle, laid bare with a single word

Dodge those eyes tempered with ice
A mask covers my other face
A face that, after the wabi-sabi of the flesh
Sneaks into another time and space

三

那些鳥兒　意念如此單純
啄食晨光　順道探望
窗前疊影枯坐的我

這是我們之間的禪
對自由的敬畏
對善念的執守

至於那偶爾撞響玻窗的喙
其實在說　嘿
可憐的老友　塵世這般嶙峋
你卻學不會飛翔

四

有些人悄無聲息的離開
淪為別人記憶的補丁
有些人無以迴避的活著
長成別人心底的陰影

我很想告訴某人　若我
剪掉讓他忌憚半生的鬍鬚
無處遁形的　就不止是
身體袒露的缺陷

III

Those birds, with such pure intent
Peck at the morning light, and stop by to visit
Me, sitting huddled in overlapping shadows by the window

This is the zen between us
Reverence for freedom
Perseverance in kindness

As for the beak that occasionally strikes the glass window
It is actually saying, Hey
Poor old friend, the mortal world is so jagged
Yet you never learn to fly

IV

Some leave without a sound
Reduced to patches in others' memories
Some live with no way to escape
Growing into shadows in others' hearts

I long to tell someone, if I
Cut off the beard that has daunted him for half his life
What will be exposed, with nowhere to hide
Is more than the flaws bared by my body

五

怕蛇　怕所有蠕行的軟體
卻又幻想褪去一身傲骨
像蛇一樣活下去

總有蛇　像寒芒淬煉的冷兵器
穿越我的夢境　肉身以及靈魂
直抵荒涼的現實

而其實　我們每個人的內心
都蜷著一條蛇　或毒或馴
或蟄伏　或出擊

當年　被剪斷的臍帶
原是穿越母親夢境的蛇
所以我像怕死去一樣
怕著那條冰冷的蛇

V

I fear snakes, fear all writhing soft-bodied things
Yet I fantasize about shedding my pride
To live like a snake

There is always a snake, like a cold weapon tempered with
sharp frost
Passing through my dreams, my flesh, and my soul
Straight to the desolate reality

And in truth, within each of us
Coils a snake—either venomous or tame
Either dormant or striking

That umbilical cord, cut off years ago
Was originally a snake that traveled through my mother's dreams
So I fear that cold snake
As I fear death itself

有關花兒的預言

一

讀不懂花兒的預言
我便以崇高的目光望你
一隻鳥從天空俯衝而下
刺穿我的掌心
你說　把心打開吧
以鳥兒的姿態綻開的花兒
便可以自由飛翔

二

牧人走後
木屋回到童話裡
一張沉重的紙上
我移植故土的山花和野草
偶爾　一隻熟悉的雲雀
飛來花叢喚我兒時的乳名

The Prophecy of the Flowers

I

Unable to understand the prophecy of flowers,
I gaze at you with lofty eyes.
A bird dives down from the sky,
Piercing my palm.
You say, "Open your heart,
And the flowers that bloom in the shape of birds
Will fly freely."

II

After the shepherd leaves,
The wooden cabin returns to the fairy tale.
On a heavy piece of paper,
I transplant the mountain flowers and wild grasses of my homeland.
Occasionally, a familiar skylark
Flies into the flowers, calling my childhood name.

三

日子水一樣流淌
於一枚七竅的鷹笛
思鄉的時候
我輕輕地吐氣
一條溪流　就彎彎曲曲
越過遠山和草地
把地平線擦得雪亮

四

風不敲門的夜晚
時間　只剩下一盞孤燈
紙上的人影　用單純的意念
反復掂量　一粒雪的重量

都在生活中突圍啊
誰指望誰　將靈魂化成舍利子
餵養你雪花一樣潔白的愛情

III

The days flow like water,
Through a seven-holed eagle flute.
When I miss home,
I gently exhale,
And a stream winds its way
Across distant mountains and fields,
Polishing the horizon to a snowy brightness.

IV

On a night when the wind does not knock,
Time is left with only a solitary lamp.
The shadow on the paper, with simple thought,
Measures over and over the weight of a single snowflake.
We are all breaking out of life,
Who expects anyone to turn their soul into a relic,
Feeding you with a love as pure as snowflakes.

五

我是打馬經過的牧童啊
鞭梢甩響的愛情　在浮光流瑩中迷了路
誰會用花的語言喚我
讓我也學會
用靈魂走路

沒有我打開的翅膀
天空開始下墜
溫衾暖帳　翼上的經卷容易受潮
我的巢穴在神祉的高度
彈簧的張力無法抵達

我背負的風水和八卦
如何借浮世的眼
生生相息

V

I am the shepherd boy passing by,
The whip cracking, love lost in the fleeting light.
Who will call me with the language of flowers,
So that I may also learn
To walk with my soul?

Without wings that I have opened,
The sky begins to fall.
The warm quilt and the scriptures on my wings easily dampen,
My nest is at the height of divinity,
Where the tension of a spring cannot reach.

The feng shui and the bagua that I carry,
How can I breathe life through the eyes of the floating world?

驚蟄（外一首）

驚蟄　每個人都在等一聲雷
越過都市的鋒芒以及所有
花朵的明媚　錚然炸響
而我想聽見的迴響
來自遼闊都市以遠
一片油菜花的蕩漾

驚蟄　春光肆無忌憚地鋪陳
春水在每個人心裡蕩漾
日子明媚得像一顆顆草莓
給我們酣暢的甜
更給我們慢性的毒

驚蟄的雷　驚醒的
不止活著的一切

The Awakening of Insects (And Another Poem)

The Awakening of Insects
Everyone is waiting for a thunderclap,
Crossing the sharp edges of the city and all
The bright flowers, with a loud, ringing burst.
But the echo I long to hear
Comes from beyond the vast city,
A ripple of rapeseed flowers in the distance.

The spring light of The Awakening of Insects spreads unchecked,
The spring water ripples in everyone's heart.
The days are as bright as strawberries,
Giving us both intoxicating sweetness,
And slowly poisoning us.

The thunder of The Awakening of Insects,
Awakens not just all that is alive.

空 境

一

這時節　薄脆的紅塵
經不住太過熾烈的陽光
氣溫不高不低　正適合
一支雪茄　不深不淺地　訴說

靈魂覆雪的男人
橫在嘴邊的鷹笛　吹瘦
時光蛻皮的生命寂靜

二

中庭裡　曾經挺立的大喬
裹一身甲冑　陷身時光困局
惟隱者修竹　偏以瘦葉逆鋒
寫意精神突圍　塵世以遠
桃花源裡住著的
都是苦難磨亮的靈魂

但只要明媚還是春天的使命
我們就可以拉開窗簾
給身披梨花的未歸人
留一盞塵世溫暖的燈

Empty Realm

I

At this time, the fragile mortal world
Cannot bear the sun's too-blazing glow
The temperature, neither high nor low, is just right
For a cigar to speak, not too deep, not too slow

A man with a soul covered in snow
Holds an eagle flute to his lips, playing thin
The silent life where time sheds its skin

II

In the courtyard, the once-tall Chinese wisteria
Clad in armor, trapped in time's snare
Only the recluse bamboo, with slender leaves defying the wind
Paints a spiritual breakout, far from the mortal care
Those who dwell in the Peach Blossom Land
Are all souls polished by suffering's hand

Yet as long as brightness remains spring's mission
We can draw back the curtain
For the unreturned one cloaked in pear blossoms
Leave a lamp, warm with mortal affection

三

這時節　適合枕著冥想
攀援樊籬　擷取夢想的翅膀
接引天光
還行屍以魂魄
還骷髏以熱血
還生命　以孤獨和尊嚴

空境之風　吹醒枝頭蓓蕾
醒來的人　早已遠赴
自己的舊石器時代
打撈熱血滾燙的人間往事
而我只能用死去的自己
背起重生

四

這時節
綿密的雨代替了人類說話
穿行在人煙荒蕪的街道
我目之所及的人世　像一枚
銜在暮色唇邊的歎息

焚一炷香　煮一壺茶
預約一場來世的雪
化解與紙筆的半生糾葛
在雨夜抵達自己的詩人
靈魂滾燙

III

At this time, it is fitting to rest in meditation
Climb the fences, pluck the wings of dream
Draw down the light of heaven
Give soul back to the walking dead
Give warm blood back to the skull
Give life back its loneliness and dignity, unbowed

The wind of the empty realm stirs the flower buds on the bough
Those who wake have long gone far
To their own Paleolithic age
To fish up the burning, warm tales of the mortal star
But I can only take my dead self
And bear the weight of rebirth, by myself

IV

At this time
Dense rain speaks in humanity's stead
Wandering the streets where human trace has fled
The world my eyes behold is like a sigh
Clutched between the lips of dusk, passing by

Light an incense stick, brew a pot of tea
Make an appointment with the snow of the next life, free
To resolve the half-life entanglement with brush and paper
A poet who reaches himself on this rainy night
Has a soul burning, bright and brighter

五

這時節
不再匆忙趕路的蓓蕾們
在潔白的時間之上
站成佛子的模樣

這是屬於你們的又一個春天
孩子　請以智慧的眼光
尋找春光深處的良人
木槿般隱忍的墨香
一縷寂靜的煙火

V

At this time
The flower buds, no longer hurrying on their way
Stand upon the white time, day by day
In the likeness of Buddha's disciples, calm and still

This is another spring that belongs to you, my child
Please look with eyes of wisdom, mild
For the kind one in the depth of spring light
The hidden fragrance of ink, enduring like hibiscus bright
And a wisp of silent smoke, soft and slight

包家巷　七十七號（組詩）

一

包家巷　七十七號
一對銀杏老夫妻　靜靜地
站在塵世之外　掉落的果實
在巷子裡濺起嬰兒的啼哭
一聲又一聲

而我要等候的消息
來自一片翅羽的響亮與歡悅

二

這些年　總有一隻鷹
為我打掃靈魂上空的雪
消弭那些晶瑩的罪孽
並坐實　度我而來的佛
其實是十月懷胎的女人

我雙手合十　騰出餘生的空
以及所有適合打坐的夜

Baojia Alley, No. 77 (A Series of Poems)

I

Baojia Alley, No. 77,
An old couple of ginkgo trees quietly
Stand outside the world. The fallen fruit
Splatters in the alley, crying like a baby,
Over and over again.

And the message I await
Comes from the loud and joyous sound of wings.

II

All these years, a hawk has
Been sweeping the snow above my soul,
Erasing those crystalline sins,
And confirming that the Buddha who came to me
Was actually the woman in the tenth month of pregnancy.
I fold my hands in prayer,

Making space for the rest of my life,
And all the nights suitable for meditation.

三

公元 2015 年 2 月 3 日
包家巷　七十七號
一朵花的綻放走漏春的行藏
以及穿越夢境的竹馬
抵達前世的消息

在詩歌裡還俗的男人
乾淨的身份　讓世界蕩漾

四

有些毒　很輕　卻深入骨髓
譬如煮字療饑的成癮　譬如
隱身中年的幻想　譬如
總是忍不住猜測奶瓶裡的度數
和在一張尿不濕裡迷路的可能性

中年人父的熱望就戮冷兵器的冷
我終與自己決裂　成為宿仇

III

On February 3rd, 2015,
Baojia Alley, No. 77,
A flower blooming reveals the secret movements of spring
And the bamboo horse crossing dreams
Brings news from a past life.

In the poetry of a man returning to the secular world,
A clean identity makes the world ripple.

IV

Some poisons are light, but they penetrate deep into the bones,
Like the addiction of words to stave off hunger,
Like the hidden fantasies of middle age,
Like always being unable to resist guessing the alcohol level in a baby bottle,
And the possibility of getting lost in a diaper.

A middle-aged father's hot expectations
Are as cold as the blade of a weapon.
I finally sever ties with myself,
Becoming a long-held enemy.

五

枯葉般捲曲的老人伸出的手
只為一餐果腹的食物
風掠而過卻又折身而返
正好撞見樹下的老人
把手中的紙幣和身體一起折疊

是日　阿彌陀佛本尊聖誕
是日　卿安問世第五天

這裡是包家巷　七十七號

V

The curled hand of an old man, like a withered leaf,
Only reaches out for a meal to fill his stomach.
The wind brushes by but turns back,
Just in time to meet the old man under the tree
Folding both the banknote and his body.

On this day, the birthday of Amitabha Buddha,
On this day, the fifth day of Qing'an's birth.

This is Baojia Alley, No. 77.

第三輯

冥想的虛無及真實性

Volume III:

The Nihility and Reality of Meditation

取珠（組詩）

一

十一樓　三十四床　靠窗
遠處　風吹皺的樓影成為雲的替身
病號服裡的我成了自己的替身
靜候　一抹刀光的驚豔
成全生命的一次起義

二

慘白　冷徹　幽閉　無菌
這神秘之處　終要見血方休
藥水覆蓋大淨的肉體之後
我腦海裡飛旋的意象
是這一生最大的菌毒

三

與水質和習慣無關　我一直堅信
體內所藏之珠　是一粒不願落塵
精神孕化的籽　見證我與內心風暴
以及蒙難文字的肝膽相照

Gathering Pearls (A Sequence of Poems)

I

On the eleventh floor, bed thirty-four, by the window,
In the distance, the wind wrinkles the shadow of buildings,
becoming a stand-in for the clouds.
In my hospital gown, I become a stand-in for myself,
Waiting for the flash of a knife's brilliance,
To fulfill the uprising of my life.

II

Pale, cold, sealed, sterile—
This mysterious place will not cease until it sees blood.
After the antiseptic covers my purified flesh,
The images spinning in my mind
Are the greatest virus of this life.

III

Unrelated to water quality or habits, I have always believed,
The pearl hidden within me is one that refuses to touch dust,
A seed of spiritual transformation,
Witnessing my inner storms
And the shared fortitude of suffering words.

四

體內　刀鋒游走的冷芒
妙到毫巔地刻畫新的秩序
體外　歸於安詳的表情和
一些不明身份的詞匯
終於有了溫暖的下落

五

鏖戰到精疲力竭的刀客
渾忘了自己帶血的處女作
他的女助手　還在驚歎手術臺上
待刀之人性感的鬍鬚和喉結
麻藥一般　沒有半點色情意味

六

於血泊中為我收拾遺珠的女人
懷揣的嬰兒　只待張口領取姓氏
逼她丟了膽兒的父親　從此以
比這落塵之珠更堅硬的文字
擊碎所有生活的苦難

IV

Within my body, the cold gleam of the blade dances,
Perfectly sketching new order.
On the outside, the expression of tranquility
And some unidentifiable words,
Finally finding a warm resting place.

V

The exhausted swordsman, after a grueling battle,
Forgets his bloodied first work.
His female assistant still marvels at the man's sensual beard and Adam's apple
On the operating table,
The anesthetic-like effect, void of any sensual implication.

VI

The woman who gathers the pearls from the bloodied battlefield for me,
Carries an unborn child, waiting to inherit a surname.
Her father, who once made her lose her courage,
Now shatters all the hardships of life
With words harder than this dust-laden pearl.

泰安古鎮

一

泰安古鎮
時間被賦予形狀
一花一葉　一磚一甌
一縷炊煙裡家的模樣
一如此刻
熟睡在我肩頭的小天使
以蝶的姿態穿越夢境
穿越逝水的徹悟
穿越忘川的決絕
所有的趕赴都只為一聲
煖朵　嚇著回來咯

二

小小孫女求抱抱　情急中
耄耋爺爺扔了拐杖　好一陣踉蹌
半生把無數山頭踩在腳下的男人
此刻　泛起在臉上褶皺裡的紅潮
嗆住了迷路的光陰

Tai'an Ancient Town

I

In Tai'an Ancient Town,
Time is given shape—
A flower, a leaf, a brick, a plaque,
A wisp of smoke reveals the form of home.
At this moment,
A little angel, sound asleep on my shoulder,
Flies through dreams in the form of a butterfly,
Crossing the realization of the passing waters,
Crossing the finality of the River of Forgetfulness.
All the journeys are just for one sound,
"Warmth, come back now!"

II

The little granddaughter asks for a hug, in haste—
The elderly grandfather tosses his cane and stumbles for a moment,
A man who has trampled countless mountain peaks beneath his feet,
Now flushed in the wrinkles of his face,
Choking on the lost time.

三

一歲半未滿的小煖朵
喜歡揪玩爸爸的鬍鬚　她不知道
為了守護這生命中最堅硬的部分
她的爸爸　付出了
不止一根骨頭的代價

四

燒烤架上的兔子和雞
四肢舒展　神態安詳
渾忘了一旁拄拐的白髮老人
攢蓄下一步的艱辛

火焰灼燒的生命之輕
拐杖敲打的生命之重
在古鎮悠遠的時光裡
清淺得濺不起一絲漣漪

III

The little "Warmth," not yet a year and a half,
Likes to tug at her father's beard. She doesn't know
That to protect the hardest part of this life,
Her father has paid
The price of more than one bone.

IV

The rabbit and chicken on the grill,
Limbs stretched, their expressions serene,
Forgetting the white-haired old man nearby,
Who has been storing up his strength for the next step.

The lightness of life, burned by flames,
The heaviness of life, tapped by a cane,
In the long and distant·time of the ancient town,
So shallow that no ripples are stirred.

五

泰安古鎮
我是坐進暗夜　自己的佛
每一縷光芒
都來自內心清澈的悲憫
何以言說涼薄
群山扯起的大氅
生息早已暖透人世

六

只有山裡人知道
每一片樹葉其實是綠色的雪花
每一瓣雪花其實是時間的魚
從泰安一路向西
梨花金頂上潔白的隱喻
昭示我的孩子　飛翔
才是空行母活著的意義
而我的每一次伏身傾聽
都有狼嚎滾過高原
留在靈魂裡的回聲

V

In Tai'an Ancient Town,
I sit in the dark night, my own Buddha.
Every ray of light
Comes from the clear compassion in my heart.
How can I speak of coldness?
The great cloak drawn up by the mountains,
Long ago warmed the human world.

VI

Only the mountain folk know,
Every leaf is truly a green snowflake,
Every petal of a snowflake is really a fish of time.
From Tai'an, heading west,
The pear blossoms on the golden peak, a pure metaphor,
Signaling to my child that flight
Is the meaning of life for the Sky-Walking Mother.
And with every bow of my head to listen,
The howl of wolves rolls across the plateau,
Leaving echoes in the soul.

暗夜如傷

一

暗夜如傷
豢養死去的理想
坐進黑暗　回到第一人稱
回到圭臬之外的秩序

二

在潔白的紙上
寫黑色的傷
直到把自己寫成
這世上唯一的光

三

從黑暗的窗口望出去
每一盞靜立的街燈
都有了美人的模樣
沿著內心發光的路
發現自己是可以飛翔的

The Dark Night, Like a Wound

I

The dark night is like a wound,
Nurturing the ideals that have died.
I sit in the dark, returning to the first person,
Returning to an order beyond the standards.

II

On a sheet of pure white paper,
I write black wounds,
Until I write myself into
The only light in this world.

III

Looking out through the dark window,
Every streetlight standing still
Takes the shape of a beautiful woman.
Along the path that glows from within,
I realize I can fly.

四

饱蘸夜的墨汁
铺月光为纸
写下的每一笔孤独
都将成为你明天的晚餐

五

闪烁的烟头
给黑夜以呼吸
肩头的灯盏
拨亮的暗黑
都源自你自己

六

灯光锋利
劈开暗夜的蚌
请以善良的名义摘取
准我以灵魂的香
赶阳光下的路

IV

Soaked in the ink of the night,
I spread moonlight as paper,
Every stroke of loneliness I write
Will become your dinner tomorrow.

V

The flickering cigarette end
Gives the night a breath.
The lamp on my shoulder
Illuminates the darkness,
All of this comes from within you.

VI

The light is sharp,
Splitting the dark night's shell.
Please, in the name of kindness, pluck it,
Allow me to take the fragrance of my soul
And walk the path under the sunlight.

七

相較於光的偽善
我更喜歡黑夜
袒露真實的陰謀
穿上暗夜蛛絲結成的袈裟
我一邊打坐　一邊
與別人的塵世決裂

八

將自己懸於暗夜之腹
像一枚胎芽回到母體
回到水的小世界
不必睜眼就可以
從容往返天地

九

天道高高在上
徒留黑夜
成為人間的鏡子
我們在裡面
看見自己的清白

VII

Compared to the hypocrisy of light,
I prefer the dark night,
Exposing the true conspiracy.
Dressed in the monk's robe woven from the night's spider silk,
I meditate, severing ties
With the mundane world of others.

VIII

I suspend myself in the belly of the dark night,
Like a bud returning to the womb,
Back to the small world of water,
No need to open my eyes to calmly travel
Between heaven and earth.

IX

The way of heaven is high above,
Leaving only the dark night
As the mirror of the world.
In it, we see
Our own innocence.

廢墟上的寫意（組詩）

一 中朝的集結令

投筆事廚的中朝先生
一把妙鏟　炒熱帝都的日子
拎一腔古道熱腸　打馬回鄉
急切間竟然忘記懷揣聖旨
而藏於集結令上的玄機
讓白河路九十九號
廢墟裡的煙火找回身份的銘牌
當所有趕赴的心情在抵達之前
溢出酒香　一句想念大家了
嗆在淚光裡的酒杯　默不作聲

二 子木的洛陽鏟

以稻粱　更以使命的名義
在活著的光陰裡盜火
在死去的光陰裡飛針
人世以外　有更飽滿的真相
每一次時空穿越後的複歸
子木先生都以嬰兒面世的虔誠
一手攥緊光陰的臍帶　一手攥緊
人世所有與溫暖有關的線索

Impression on the Ruins (A Series of Poems)

I. The Call to Gather from Zhongchao

The gentleman from Zhongchao,
Who swapped his pen for the kitchen,
With a clever spatula, stir-fries the days of the imperial capital.
He lifts a heart full of ancient passion and rides back to his homeland.
In his haste, he forgets the imperial decree,
Yet the hidden secrets in the order of the gathering
Lead the smoky ruins of No. 99, Baihe Road,
To reclaim their identity with a nameplate.
Before all hearts arrive,
The scent of wine spills over,
A simple, "I've missed you all,"
Suffocating in the tear-filled glass, silent.

II. The Luoyang Spade of Zimu

With rice and millet, And in the name of mission,
He steals fire in the living moments,
And weaves needles in the dead hours.
Beyond the human world, There is a more complete truth.
Every time he returns after a space-time journey,
Mr. Zimu emerges with the devotion of a newborn,
One hand holding the umbilical cord of time,
The other grasping all the clues related to warmth in the human world.

三 紀阿哥的煙斗

以毫鋒與墨色的至柔
淬寫有血有肉的江湖以及男兒有骨
銀髮不是因為輕慢
惟因敬畏而生的倔強
書道尚勤 心道尚簡
歧途多美妙 離舍是徹悟
高懸于顯赫祖譜之上的煙鍋
如今被握在手上 熄了火
以煙霧之輕如何匹敵一支筆
對活著的描述及進退自如

四 牧山的袈裟

紙上行雲 吐盡思想風暴
筆走龍蛇 降縛內心魔獸
之後 且打坐 且入定
並以慈悲為懷的名義
卸去重裝甲冑 卸去鋼筋鐵骨
回到一部經書的心臟
回到關於男人如山的所有隱喻
以及柔軟的本質
給靈魂穿上袈裟的男人
暢飲之前的笑容正好 52 度

III. The Smoking Pipe of Brother Ji

With the sharpness of a fine brush and the softness of ink,
He writes of the flesh-and-bone world of the rivers and lakes, of men with backbone.
Silver hair is not due to neglect,
But the stubbornness born of reverence.
Calligraphy demands diligence,
The heart demands simplicity.
Many paths are beautiful,
Leaving the house is enlightenment.
The smoking pipe, once high upon the illustrious family tree,
Now rests in his hand, extinguished.
How could the lightness of smoke match the weight of a pen,
In describing life and navigating between actions and restraint?

IV. The Monk's Robe of Mushan

Clouds move on paper, Thought storms are expelled.
The brush dances like dragons and snakes,
Binding the inner demons. Then, sit in meditation, enter tranquility,
And in the name of compassion,
Lay down the heavy armor, the iron bones,
Return to the heart of a scripture,
Back to all the metaphors of men as mountains,
And their soft essence.
The man who dresses his soul in the monk's robe
Drinks deeply, smiling just before the perfect 52-degree sip.

五 公子的布衣

頭上泰山待奉　膝下嬰幼待哺
身前有雷區　身後有鞭子
既然俯仰都充滿危機和懸念
骨殖的捐付就成為必然的成本
只是我早已習慣麥芒和詩歌的毒
以及命運以血脈的遙遠許諾
習慣扛著肩上奶香趕明天的路
以生命之輕　以幸福之重
從此與立地成佛
只差一步

V. The Common Clothes of the Young Master

Above my head, the mountain waits to be served,
At my feet, infants wait to be nourished.
Before me, there are minefields; behind, there are whips.
Since both humility and grandeur are full of danger and suspense,
The donation of bone and marrow becomes inevitable.
Yet, I have long been accustomed to the poison of wheat glumes and poetry,
And the distant promises of fate through the bloodline.
Accustomed to carrying the scent of milk on my shoulders,
Rushing toward tomorrow's path,
With the lightness of life and the weight of happiness,
From this moment, only one step remains
To achieve enlightenment.

編鐘王朝

尊盤已覆　酒觚已傾
曾侯乙你的子民安在
雲珠與棠玉　靈覺與肉身
抽走哪一根骨頭
痛肉身更痛社稷

空棺欲睡　君王不歸
蟠龍欲遊　時光靜止
一鐘雙音　五聲七宮
終謀不盡盛世一場
空懸木椌荒了珠玉的愛戀

樂音五度暖了心腸
兵戈零下冷了江山
始於宮的盛宴
如何止於羽的輕賤
鳳舞天下　一曲沸騰
即是萬歲

你有金聲玉振　合瓦秘技
我有民間說唱　煙火搖滾
作為君王　兩年多年
你翻不過一道殘破城牆
我是布衣　一個時辰
便已輕描淡寫了楚河漢界

The Zhou Dynasty Bell

The revered plate has already overturned, the wine vessel already spilled,
Where are the people of Lord Chang's reign now?
Cloud pearls and tang jade, spirit and flesh,
Which bone have you removed?
The body aches, and so does the realm.

The empty coffin seeks rest, the king does not return,
The coiled dragon yearns to move, while time stands still.
One bell with two sounds, five tones and seven notes,
In the end, the grand era was never fully planned,
The wooden mallet hangs in the air, the love of pearls and jade lies in ruins.

The melody of five notes warms the heart,
While the coldness of war chills the land,
Beginning with the grand feast of the palace,
How does it end with the triviality of feathers?
The phoenix dances across the world, a song of boiling fervor,
And that, indeed, is eternal.

You have the golden sound and the jade vibration, the secret art of the tiles,
I have the folk tales and the fireworks rock 'n' roll.
As a king, two years or many more,
You cannot cross a single broken city wall,
I am a commoner, and in one hour,
I have already casually drawn the boundary between Chu and Han.

王道猙獰　你沉默如讖
禮樂清歡　你懸秘於鐘
王的魂已杳　樂的靈尤暖
重要的不是江山落入誰手
而是你高蹈音樂之上的靈魂
是否已在盛世落草為寇

The way of the king is ferocious, and you remain silent like an omen,
The rituals and music are clear and joyous,
You remain hidden in the bell,
The soul of the king is long gone, but the spirit of music still warms.
What matters is not who holds the empire,
But whether your soul, transcending the music,
Has become a bandit in this prosperous world.

被一張紙劃傷

一 被一張紙劃傷

一頁紙的邊緣竟然鋒利如刀
劃傷我的手指 沒有流血
只是打開書的念頭痛了一下

眼睛畏縮地跟著跳了跳
趕緊合上書 密封一個不詳徵兆
可我還是聽見書裡胎動的聲音

書裡 不過是千年的唐風宋韻
封面也只是一粒今時塵埃
開合之間 紙的鋒芒
割裂了我們的思維慣性

Scratched by a Piece of Paper

I. Scratched by a Piece of Paper

The edge of a page is as sharp as a blade,
It scratches my finger, but no blood flows.
Only the thought of opening the book hurts a little.

My eyes flinch, and they jump,
Quickly I close the book, sealing an ominous sign.
But I still hear the sound of fetal movement within the pages.

Inside the book, it's just the thousand-year-old Tang wind and
Song melodies.
The cover, merely a speck of dust from this time.
Between opening and closing,
The sharpness of the paper
Rips apart our habitual thoughts.

二 在相片裡定居

仿佛該是瓜熟蒂落了
採摘既然不是罪過
我的恐懼何來

翻越戒指的柵欄
婚姻的面目其實一目了然
只是我內心有魔　靈魂如獸

我渴望的愛情
猙獰且帶有致命的劇毒
不在灰燼裡重生　就在燦爛中死

在走進墳墓以前
請讓我先死在愛情裡
並在一組照片裡
以一隻鷹或狼飛翔或奔突的姿勢
定居人類婚姻生活

II. Settling in a Photograph

It seems like the melon should be ripe,
And picking it isn't a crime.
But where does my fear come from?

Climbing over the fence of the ring,
Marriage's true face is actually clear.
Yet inside me, there's a demon, and my soul is a beast.

The love I long for,
Is fierce and carries deadly poison.
It will either be reborn from the ashes or die in the brilliance.

Before I walk into the grave,
Let me die first in love,
And in a photograph,
Let me settle, soaring like an eagle or running like a wolf,
In the posture of human marriage.

三 懷念一個人

一間沒有燈光的屋子
一段叫做《紅》的音樂
水霧般 飄繞流轉

一根煙在手裡 一根在煙缸裡
一杯酒在唇邊 另一杯在茶几上
屋子裡沒人

燈光複製了整個城市
卻複製不了一段
塵世和天堂臨界的懷念

屋子裡沒人 音樂響著
煙在同時燃燒著
酒杯在同時退潮

嘿 我說 傻女孩 你懷念的人
他不在屋子裡 也不在天堂
不信你就把燈點亮

III. Missing a Person

A room without light,
A piece of music called "Red,"
Floating like mist, turning and swirling.

A cigarette in my hand, one in the ashtray,
A cup of wine by my lips, another on the table.
There's no one in the room.

The light has replicated the entire city,
But it cannot replicate
A nostalgia on the border between the mortal world and heaven.

The room is empty, the music plays,
The smoke burns simultaneously,
The wine cup simultaneously recedes.

Hey, I say, silly girl, the one you miss,
He's neither in the room nor in heaven.
If you don't believe me, just turn on the light.

四　人這輩子

患糖尿病的父親藥吃完了
飯量大增　醫生早叮囑
這病不能吃太多

高原工作幾十年的父親
退休工資不夠買自己吃的藥
醫療保險又嫌他人老病重

給父親買藥我心情很矛盾
吃了藥的父親吃不飽肚子
吃飽肚子以後或許就不用再吃藥

人這輩子　苦熬數十寒暑
只不過要換得一餐清秋
我垂暮的父親　到了晚年
他竟然不敢吃飽

IV. This Life

My father, with diabetes, has run out of his medicine,
His appetite has increased. The doctor warned early on,
Not to eat too much.

Father, who worked on the plateau for decades,
His pension isn't enough to buy his own medicine,
Medical insurance finds him too old and too sick.

Buying medicine for my father, I feel conflicted,
The father who takes the medicine still can't fill his stomach,
Once his stomach is full, perhaps he won't need the medicine anymore.

In this life, after enduring dozens of cold winters and hot summers,
All one seeks is a simple meal in the clear autumn.
My aging father, in his later years,
He dares not eat his fill.

五 上帝是公平的

酒足飯飽　桌上的辣子雞還剩了大半
打包給小應帶回去
有人提議

打好的包放在車座的腳墊上
一路上　車主總是擔心
塑料袋破了會弄髒自己的車

每次小應都彎腰抬起沉重的金屬杆
從別人手裡接過打包的剩菜
低頭道謝

這次也不例外　接過豐盛的晚餐
小應趕緊扯出身後的女兒
讓謝謝送菜的阿姨

看著小女孩漂亮的臉蛋兒
阿姨突然感慨
上帝是公平的

V. God is Fair

After a hearty meal, there's still a large portion of spicy chicken on the table,
It's packed for Xiaoying to take home.
Someone suggests it,

The packed food is placed on the floor mat of the car,
Along the way, the driver worries,
That the plastic bag will tear and dirty the car.

Each time, Xiaoying bends down to lift the heavy metal rod,
Takes the leftovers from someone's hands,
And thanks them.

This time is no exception. After taking the sumptuous dinner,
Xiaoying quickly pulls out his daughter from behind,
To have her thank the aunt who delivered the food.

Looking at the little girl's beautiful face,
The aunt suddenly sighs,
"God is fair."

俯仰之間的呈現

一 關於我

不會水的我從小就奔跑在驚濤駭浪中
西部堅硬的風 磨亮我的眼睛
我看見 山峰其實是無比鋒利的波浪
為了生存 鳥類才長著翅膀

我沒有翅膀 我只能奔跑 不停地奔跑
溫情且母性的高原陽光 在我單薄稚嫩的身體裡
種植溫暖的花瓣 並把指印
深深地摁進我向陽的額頭

暗夜花開 神在高處提著星燈趕路
我用冰涼的雪花覆蓋年輕的蒼茫
理想在牧鞭上蔥鬱
倥傯歲月的殤 羈旅的況味
擠出歲月的眼睛
就落進我的酒杯

零度以上 我醉了
零度以下 酒杯碎了

The Presentation Between Looking Up and Looking Down

I. About Me

I, who cannot swim, have been running in turbulent waves since childhood.
The hard winds of the West sharpened my eyes.
I saw that mountains are, in fact, razor-sharp waves.
Birds only have wings to survive.

I have no wings. I can only run—run endlessly.
The tender, maternal sunlight of the plateau plants warm petals in my thin, youthful body,
Pressing the imprint of my fingers deeply into my sun-facing forehead.

In the dark night, flowers bloom.
God holds a star lantern, hurrying along.
I cover my young, vast sky with cold snowflakes.
Ideals grow lush on the shepherd's whip.
The wounds of fleeting years, the flavor of wandering,
Squeeze out the eyes of time,
And they fall into my wine glass.

Above zero, I am drunk.
Below zero, the wine glass shatters.

二 關於愛情

人們口中沉重得無以復加的愛情
被我輕描淡寫地裝在一個帆布書包裡
寫禿了無數支鉛筆和鋼筆 紙上的覆雪
始終無法燃燒一個屬我 燦爛的春天

坐等的日子 我偎身在愛情的邊緣取暖
去歲秋草 驛路梅花 總有芳香指引
心漂得久了 腳步開始脫水
這詩意且危險的旅程 很容易就走火入魔

似仙 衣衫飄袂間就抖落一場風花雪月
似巫 一個咒語就鎖住地老天荒
我們是人 只能用一個欲望覆蓋另一個欲望
用今天的煙火餵養明天的愛情

在塵世 布衣荊釵的愛情
是盛在土瓷碗裡的孟婆湯
一飲而盡 就是逝水忘川
一口一口地喝 才是天長地久

II. About Love

The heavy love, endlessly overwhelming in people's mouths,
I lightly pack it into a canvas backpack,
Countless pencils and fountain pens wear down, the snow on paper
Still cannot burn a spring that belongs to me—bright and dazzling.

On the days of waiting, I snuggle at love's edge to warm myself.
Last autumn's grasses, the plum blossoms on the post-road,
There is always fragrance to guide me.
After my heart drifts for too long, my steps begin to dehydrate.
This poetic yet dangerous journey easily spirals into obsession.

Like an immortal, my robes fluttering, shaking off a scene of wind, flowers, snow, and moon.
Like a witch, a single incantation locks time, making the world age.
We are humans, and can only cover one desire with another,
Feed tomorrow's love with today's fireworks.

In the mortal world, the love of commoners,
Is the soup of the Meng Po that rests in an earthen bowl.
One sip, and it is the River of Forgetfulness.
One sip at a time, and that is eternity.

三 關於事業

事業　一個讓我們多麼羞愧的字眼
就為了給一隻碗鑲上華麗的金邊
我們用了多少粉飾的辭藻
來包裝胃囊裡的米粒和油膩

我們都是用飽嗝給生命打更的人
靠夢囈與生活拉近距離
用飯碗上的缺口接住別人的恥笑
用肉體的缺口　恥笑別人的生活

我們渴望一種物理的高度
懸置命運未葡的情節　在密閉的籠中
俯瞰低處的油畫　和畫上逃逸的煙火
這樣的高度　投擲的陰影
最適合掩蓋生活的瘡疤

而我　堅硬且沒有韌性的膝
不適合沿頌詞的高度攀緣
惟有前行　在風的浸潤和陽光的耳語中
放牧身心　並以國粹的精神
任後現代場景的切割與置換

生活和城市　每天都在增加新的高度
從高處飄墜的頭顱　落不進生活的碗
而我的視線　始終與一隻碗平行

III. About Career

Career—what an utterly shameful word,
Just to adorn a bowl with a fancy golden rim,
How many decorated words we use
To wrap up the rice grains and greasy oil in our stomachs.

We all give life its toll with full bellies,
Pulling closer dreams and daily life with our sleep-talking,
Catching others' mocking laughter in the gap of our bowls,
And mocking others' lives through the gaps in our own flesh.

We long for a physical height,
Suspending the unwritten plots of fate in a closed cage,
Overlooking the oil paintings below and the fireworks escaping the canvas.
This height, with its cast shadow,
Is perfect for hiding the scars of life.

But I, with knees that are hard but lacking in flexibility,
Am unfit to climb to the heights of praises.
All I can do is move forward,
Drenched by the wind and whispered by the sunlight,
Grazing both body and soul,
And, with the spirit of national heritage,
Let the cutting and replacement of postmodern scenes come.

Life and cities are always increasing new heights.
The head that falls from a great height
Cannot land in the bowl of life.
And my gaze always remains parallel to the bowl.

恍 惚

一

收藏了太多的夜
我空洞的眼神 開始怕光
怕輕薄的明亮之後
黑色的毒

二

很想閉上眼睛
額角的神經卻無休止的痙攣
一下 兩下 三下
我默數的聲音
讓夜色露出詭秘的快意

三

一隻貓的叫聲在左耳
另一隻貓的叫聲在右耳
我憋在心裡的嘶叫
溺死在黑夜的獰笑裡
於是 我整晚都在詛咒
那該死的耗子
一定是因為偷香忘記了覓食

Daze

I

I've collected too many nights,
My hollow eyes begin to fear the light,
Afraid that after the thin brightness,
The black poison will follow.

II

I want to close my eyes,
But the nerves at my temples keep twitching endlessly,
One twitch, two, three,
The sound of my silent counting
Reveals the eerie delight of the night.

III

A cat's meow in my left ear,
Another cat's meow in my right ear,
The hissing I keep inside
Drowns in the sinister laughter of the dark.
So, I curse all night,
That damn rat,
It must have forgotten to forage, distracted by its stolen scent.

四

闪念 以暴力的美学狂轰滥炸
我却不能把自己站成一棵树
白日里人一样走路的狗
夜里狗一样蜷缩的人
所有的忧思不过是
一只碗的盈缺

五

我知道这是惩罚
任何探寻的想像都是对真相地轻薄
通宵闭不上眼睛的罪人
给不安的灵魂缝制的嫁衣
始终找不到合适的纽扣

六

前世为狼 我不能用血腥的语气数绵羊
今生为奴 童话里的星子
远逸在遥不可及的高度
做三生之外善良的鬼吧
经过你们美丽的梦境
我绝不发出半点声响

IV

A flash of thought, a violent beauty, bombarding everything,
Yet I cannot make myself stand like a tree,
A dog walking like a human by day,
A human curling up like a dog by night,
All my worries are just
The waxing and waning of a bowl.

V

I know this is punishment,
Any pursuit of imagination is a shallowness toward truth,
The sinner who cannot close his eyes all night,
Sewing the bridal gown for an uneasy soul,
Always unable to find the right button.

VI

In my past life, I was a wolf, I cannot count sheep in bloody tones,
In this life, I am a slave, the stars in fairytales
Drift far away, at an unreachable height.
Let me be a kind ghost beyond three lives,
Passing through your beautiful dreams,
I will make no sound.

七

睜著眼走過黑夜 是誰
不小心撥錯了燈盞
把我燒死在美麗的光亮裡
當我魂兒一樣經過白晝
我可以不再有愛
不再有恨麼
如此 讓我睡吧
我可以不再要求見到光明

八

這城市 該熄的燈都熄了
該來的夢都來了
多圓滿的夜晚呵
剩我在一張床上的漂泊
只一隻蟑螂陪伴

九

睡吧 整個世界都睡了
睡不著也請閉上眼睛
穿越黑夜的
不是夢境 便是死亡

VII

Who walks through the dark with eyes open,
Carelessly turns the lamp wrong,
And burns me alive in its beautiful light?
When my soul drifts through the daylight,
Can I be without love,
Without hate?
Let me sleep then,
I ask no more to see the light.

VIII

In this city, the lights that should go out have gone out,
The dreams that should come have come,
What a perfect night,
And I am left adrift on a bed,
Only a cockroach as my companion.

IX

Sleep, the whole world is asleep,
If you cannot sleep, please close your eyes,
What crosses the dark,
Is not a dream, but death.

十

在生命耗盡之前
請給我一粒安魂的藥
讓我保留一絲生命的豐潤
作為最後的感恩
那些曾經照亮過我
美麗的風景

X

Before life is used up,
Please give me a pill for the soul,
So I may preserve a bit of life's fullness,
As the final gratitude,
For those beautiful scenes
That once lit my way.

節骨眼上的詩意

一

一隻白淨且尊貴的手掌攤開
來吧 我的螞蟻 我掌紋的迷宮
藏著你的命運

用你的爬行來滿足我嗜癢的怪癖
舒服的時候 我的掌心攤得很直
不舒服的時候 我就把手心攥緊

我是你命運的巫師
而你 是無法逃離豢養的小螞蟻

二

改制分家了
火山口上的觀景臺上
忙著找座位的人 頭破了
股動脈卻異常堅韌

火山底部 風暴的中心
有人宣誓 有人倒戈
有人祈禱 有人吞吃火藥
你問我在幹什麼 嘿嘿
我坐在時間的刀刃上
寫第 190 首詩歌

The Poetic Moment at the Crucial Point

I

A white, noble hand opens wide,
Come, my ants, the labyrinth of my palm
Holds your fate.

Use your crawling to satisfy my itch,
When you're comfortable, my palm stays flat,
When you're not, I clench it tight.

I am the sorcerer of your fate,
And you are the small ant, helpless and bred.

II

The reorganization has split us,
On the observation deck of the volcano,
People scrambling for a seat, their heads cracked,
Yet their veins are oddly resilient.

At the base of the volcano, in the center of the storm,
Some swear allegiance, some betray,
Some pray, some swallow gunpowder,
You ask me what I'm doing—heh heh,
I sit on the edge of time's blade,
Writing the 190th poem.

三

有好心人勸　打個電話給某某
他不是一直都很賞識你嗎
這節骨眼上　面子
比詩歌還不值錢

我又不是守城的元帥　何必幻想
撫生命的絕唱於破城的箭雨
還是留住臉皮吧
還得繼續　從這城門
進進出出啊

你們去沖吧　殺吧　搶吧　鬥吧
我等著用詩歌盛斂你們
噴濺的血光和支離的肉屑
完成最後的詩意

四

早知道馬上會成為上下級
不如當初就戴上面具
以後　怎麼好拉下臉皮

生活中我們是朋友啊　除了老婆
什麼東西都各分一半
可屁股兩半　一個位子
該怎麼分

III

A well-meaning person advises me:
"Call someone, don't they always appreciate you?"
At this crucial moment,
Face is worth less than poetry.

I'm not the general defending a city,
Why fantasize about stroking life's final song
In the storm of broken arrows?
Let's keep the face intact,
After all, I still need to pass through these gates.

Go on, rush, kill, rob, fight,
I'll wait to collect your splattered blood and scattered flesh
With poetry,
To complete the final poetic gesture.

IV

Had I known I'd soon become a superior or subordinate,
I would've worn a mask from the start.
Now, how can I lower my face?

In life, we are friends, except for wives,
Everything else is divided in half,
But the two halves of a butt—
How do you divide that?

五

終於　還是有些傷感
門牌號　鐵皮櫃　積滿塵垢的
沙發　茶几　電視機　辦公桌和轉椅
那麼忠貞地守護　浸透我
體味和氣息的光陰

只是那只張著血盆大口的煙灰缸
不露聲色　吞吃的煙頭
連結起來　早超出了
我生命的長度

日光燈還是不改初衷的明亮
可我思想的帷幕已經徐徐拉上
今天的陽光很好　只是
它會等到我下班嗎

鎖好這扇門以後
如果電話鈴響　接聽的
是我遺留的心情　當然
你也可以留言

V

Finally, there's a bit of sadness,
The doorplate number, the metal cabinet,
The sofa, coffee table, TV, office desk, and swivel chair,
All loyally guarding the time soaked with my scent and aura.

Yet, the ashtray with its wide, blood-red mouth
Silently devours cigarette butts,
Which, when connected, exceed
The length of my life.

The fluorescent light remains as bright as ever,
But the curtain of my thoughts slowly draws shut,
Today's sunlight is wonderful,
But will it wait for me to finish work?

After locking the door,
If the phone rings,
It will be my lingering emotions on the line,
Of course, you can leave a message.

敬畏白色

一 敬畏白色

靜靜地躺著　白色的屋子
白色的床　白色的人
我在等　片刻以後
以一灘粘稠溫熱的殷紅
完成敬畏的禮儀

手術刀　止血鉗冰涼的聲音
封凍的毛孔　汗沒有出路
冷硬如鐵的身體
心跳無力突圍

金屬的鋒利切割的意識
沒有痛楚　飲血的白手套
從容撩開地獄的黑紗

敬畏白色吧　脆弱的生命
流不出太多的紅
一個蒼老的聲音
遊蕩了幾十年

Reverence for White

I. Reverence for White

Lying quietly, in a white room,
A white bed, white people,
I wait, after a moment,
To complete the ritual of reverence
With a pool of viscous, warm crimson.

The sound of a scalpel, a cold hemostat,
Frozen pores, sweat with no escape,
A body as rigid as iron,
The heartbeat struggles to break free.

The sharpness of metal cuts through consciousness,
No pain, the blood-stained white gloves
Leisurely lift the veil of hell.

Reverence for white, fragile life,
Not much red can spill out,
An aged voice
Wanders for decades.

二 無法跨越的界點

醫生說 這次流血事件
早該發生在二十多年前
無數次脹裂的傷口
回旋上帝冷酷的語氣

從一個孩子長成男人
其實是跨越了一道傷口
填滿並包裝傷口的
只是原罪的欲望

刀鋒可以劃開包裝
卻劃不開結痂的欲念
長成陰影的痛
只能一生背負

該如何回到兒時的潔白
睜眼躲開的所有有色情節
都會在睡夢中醒來
像死神的獠牙 撕咬黑夜

天明 因稚嫩童聲的召喚
渺然且遙遠 但我蘇醒的意義
因傷而崇高
因痛而偉大

II. The Uncrossable Boundary

The doctor says, this bleeding event
Should have happened over twenty years ago,
Countless ruptured wounds,
Echoing the cold voice of God.

From a child to a man,
In truth, I crossed a wound,
The wound filled and packaged
By the desire of original sin.

The blade can cut the package,
But cannot sever the scabbed desire,
The pain that grows into shadow
Can only be carried for life.

How to return to the purity of childhood?
The erotic plots I once dodged with open eyes
Will wake up in my dreams,
Like the fangs of death, tearing through the dark.

At dawn, summoned by the innocent voice of a child,
Faint and distant, but the meaning of my awakening
Is elevated by the wound,
Made great by the pain.

三 傷在下半生

有人問我傷在哪裡
我回答 傷在下半生

上半生 活在一道傷口裡
下半生 留一道傷口
讓我的孩子活

我的孩子 也一定會降生於
一間白色的屋子
一張白色的床上
那一灘粘稠的殷紅

我迫不及待想告訴他
黑暗並不可怕
但一定要敬畏白色

天氣太熱 我沒有食欲
但傷口很饑餓
空調的房間太冷
文字沒有生機 我等待的
下一個傷口
卻無比鮮活

III. The Wound of the Second Half of Life

Someone asks me, where is the wound?
I reply, the wound is in the second half of life.

In the first half of life,
I lived inside a wound,
In the second half, I leave a wound
For my child to live.

My child will surely be born
In a white room,
On a white bed,
With that pool of viscous crimson.

I can't wait to tell him,
The darkness is not to be feared,
But we must always revere white.

The weather is too hot, I have no appetite,
But the wound is very hungry,
The air-conditioned room is too cold,
The words have no life, I wait for
The next wound,
Which is incredibly vivid.

靈魂的一次謝幕

一

此刻的我　端坐於辦公桌前
想像　如刃的四壁
如何分割屬我的自由

厚積的塵垢　以怎樣的方式
浸蝕了我的行走和呼吸

很少開啟的窗戶下
盆花意外的茁壯
茶垢和痰漬　也可以佐證
一種生命的堅韌

空調把窗外的陽光化成水
我卻在恒溫的水質世界裡
脫水枯萎

這屋子裡的一切都和我緊密相關
但一切都不屬我
好在　我還可以用潔淨的十指
敲打出骨質和品節的硬度

A Curtain Call for the Soul

I

At this moment, I sit at my desk,
Imagining how the sharp four walls
Divide the freedom that belongs to me.

The accumulated dust—
In what way has it eroded my walking and my breath?

Under the rarely opened window,
The potted plants grow unexpectedly strong,
Tea stains and phlegm marks also attest
To a kind of resilience in life.

The air conditioner turns the sunlight outside into water,
But I wither away in this constant-temperature world,
Dehydrated and dried out.

Everything in this room is intimately related to me,
But nothing belongs to me.
Luckily, I can still use my clean ten fingers
To strike the hardness of bones and the integrity of character.

二

煙盒裡邊剩最後一支煙
而我 已經好幾天寫不出東西

口袋裡邊剩五塊五毛錢
我抽的煙需要四倍這樣的數

屬我的錢 銀行替我保存著
我想抽的煙 商店老闆替我保存著

沒有錢買不到煙 沒有煙寫不出東西
寫不出東西 我彷彿已經死去

死去的我 寫過的東西可能變成遺言
那些煙蒂也可能證明我是被自己謀殺的
至於那些存在銀行裡的錢
找不到繼承的人

II

There's only one cigarette left in the pack,
Yet I haven't been able to write anything for days.

There are five and a half yuan in my pocket,
But the cigarette I want needs four times that amount.

The money that belongs to me is kept by the bank,
The cigarettes I want are kept by the shopkeeper.

Without money, I can't buy cigarettes;
Without cigarettes, I can't write.
If I can't write, it's as if I've already died.

The dead me—the things I've written may become my will.
Those cigarette butts might prove that I murdered myself.
As for the money in the bank,
There's no one to inherit it.

三

門也是種面具　左右
我和陽光接觸的時間

門也是極其鋒利的　當我
從一扇門走入另另一扇門
就已經再一次完成
自己對自己的憑弔

一種眼神可以逼彎膝蓋
一種語氣可以凍僵血肉
不是陽光下的行走
身體和靈魂不在同一高度

很多的時候　是猿猴的遺傳基因
讓我們在現實的世界裡
脫胎換骨　誰說
尾巴的功能只是用來調節
身體行走的平衡

II

The door is also a kind of mask,
The time I spend with sunlight is measured by its sides.

The door is also extremely sharp—when I
Walk through one door into another,
I have once again completed
A mourning of myself.

A certain look can bend the knee,
A certain tone can freeze the flesh.
It's not walking under the sunlight—
The body and the soul are not on the same plane.

Often, it's the inherited genes of monkeys
That allow us to transform in the real world.
Who said the tail's function is only to balance
The body's movement?

四

辦公室樓層的高度在不斷增加
我的身高卻遵循了水流的規律

薪水也越來越高 地心的吸引力
卻只在我的頭皮產生作用

寫的文件越來越厚 剩下的最後一張紙
是自己的臉皮

朋友越來越多 發現唯一的敵人
原來是自己

IV

The height of the office floors keeps increasing,
But my own height follows the law of water.

My salary keeps getting higher,
But the gravitational pull of the earth
Only affects my scalp.

The documents I write are getting thicker,
The last piece of paper left
Is my own face.

I have more and more friends,
But I discover that my only enemy
Is myself.

五

道德的門虛掩的時候 我正激蕩著詩意
生命之重全部落於筆尖的時候
我的墮落也很徹底

淪陷紅塵的我 幻想用前世
一粒雪的光芒點燃案前紙上的青燈
給釘在牆上的歲月
編織一件如螢的羽衣

敏感如我 常以眼淚硌傷生活的堅硬
清高如我 在紙箋上淪落成隱君子
細膩如我 活著只是一個卑微的動詞

靈魂 經歷了太多的謝幕以後
現在的我已經成了植物人
只剩下了呼吸
和維持呼吸的欲望

如果植物人的大腦裡也有夢境
那我 前世一定是夢雪的書生
今生 我註定要打開胸膛
讓你看清楚 戀雪
是我中毒的唯一癥結

V

When the door of morality is slightly ajar,
I am stirring with poetic thoughts.
When the weight of life rests entirely on the tip of my pen,
My fall from grace is complete.

Falling into the red dust, I fantasize about using a past life
To ignite the green light on the paper in front of me
With the glow of a snowflake,
To weave a coat of fireflies for the years pinned to the wall.

Sensitive as I am, I often hurt the hardness of life
With my tears. Noble as I am, I have fallen into the role of a
humble recluse on paper.
Delicate as I am, I am nothing more than a humble verb in life.

The soul, after too many curtain calls,
Has now become a vegetative person.
There's only breathing left,
And the desire to maintain that breath.

If a vegetative brain also dreams,
Then I must have been a scholar who dreamed of snow in my
past life.
In this life, I am destined to open my chest,
To let you see clearly, That loving snow
Is the only symptom of my poisoning.

裸　傷

一

我實在記不清破土的日期
這墓 完工於 2008 年 6 月 30 日
鑽進去　我並不選擇躺下
伏案　是我遺世最後的姿態
此人無狀　拒簽命運回執

二

很多面孔　比這季節花兒更豔
很多語氣　比這夏風更暖
可這是上蒼錯誤佈置
一個罹患的年輪

這震後人間　只需生的快感
寫詩人作為禮物收下的痛楚
是一味多麼深刻的良藥
從此失傳

Bare Wounds

I

I can't quite remember the date when the earth broke open,
This grave was finished on June 30, 2008.
When I crawled in, I didn't choose to lie down,
Bowing over my desk—this was my final posture.
This person is without form, rejecting destiny's receipt.

II

Many faces are brighter than flowers this season,
Many voices warmer than the summer breeze.
But this is the mistake of the heavens,
A year of affliction bestowed upon me.

In this post-earthquake world, all that is needed is the thrill of survival,
The pain that the poet receives as a gift—
Such a deeply effective medicine,
Now lost forever.

三

痛苦的時候我的詩歌很甜
快樂的時候我的詩歌很苦
我趕著詩歌去文字的墳墓
把自己逼成這世間的孤魂野鬼

某日　心血來潮
決定把詩歌寫成演講稿
曾經忠實的文字卻拒絕
翻越一座座高聳的牌坊

四

辦公室裡的君子蘭長出兩片新葉
離開花的時間越來越近
初葉上的傷口也越來越大

固守傷痛　執意抵達花期
這陪伴我兩年多的花兒
一直複製我的命運
卻不給我任何暗示

III

When I'm in pain, my poems taste sweet,
When I'm happy, my poems turn bitter.
I rush to the poet's tomb,
Pushing myself into this world of wandering souls and ghosts.

One day, in a moment of whim,
I decided to turn my poems into a speech.
But the once loyal words refuse,
Scaling high archways that stand in my way.

IV

In my office, the "peace lily" grows two new leaves,
Its time to bloom draws nearer.
The wounds on its first leaves grow larger.

Clinging to pain, it stubbornly reaches its flowering time,
This flower, which has accompanied me for over two years,
Has always mirrored my fate,
Yet offers no hint.

五

一顆皸裂病牙 讓我有機會
聽見褪去袈裟後的夜說渴
於是 我便毫無保留
奉獻了所有疼痛

恍然驚覺 太陽已經很老了
其實是面具鍍亮的白晝
我必須懂得保護一顆堅硬的牙
比保護脆弱的心臟更重要

六

輸得很慘 但我無法悲傷
既然選擇賤賣 尊嚴
只是用來承接一根草簽的重量
就像這下市的玫瑰
只能在澡盆裡回味曾經的飄逸
不再與風情有關

更殘忍的是 背上的草簽
被人當作瘋子的行為藝術

V

A cracked, diseased tooth gives me a chance
To hear the night thirsting after its robes.
And so, without reserve,
I offered all my pain.

Suddenly, I realized—
The sun had grown old.
It was just the mask of bright daylight.
I must protect a hard tooth,
More so than a fragile heart.

VI

I lost terribly, but I can't mourn.
Since I chose to cheaply sell my dignity,
It's only there to bear the weight of a grass stick.
Like these roses, once off the market,
They can only savor their past elegance in the bathtub,
No longer related to charm.

What's more cruel,
Is that the stick on my back,
Has been called a madman's performance art.

七

作為悲情典範
所有傾情演出並不為喝彩與掌聲
只為贏得對手的尊重

請在小提琴深刻的光芒裡
原諒我退場的言不由衷
落幕之後　我再度盛開
依然是拒絕採摘的罌粟

八

我必須快樂起來　這震後大地
花兒依舊單純地開放
沒有一絲雜念

如果凋零不是最後疼痛
能說哪一種花兒最美嗎
我不能開花　但可以著一身新妝
赴一場別人的盛宴　自己的殤
並告訴自己　從此你有了
花兒一樣單純的快樂

VII

As a tragic example,
All the heartfelt performances are not for applause or cheers,
But to win the respect of my opponents.
Please, in the violin's profound light,
Forgive my unspoken retreat.

After the curtain falls,
I bloom once more,
Still the unpicked poppy,
Refusing to be harvested.

VIII

I must learn to be happy again,
This world after the quake,
Flowers still bloom purely,
Without a trace of impurity.

If wilting isn't the final pain,
Which flower can truly be called the most beautiful?
I cannot bloom, but I can wear a new dress,
Attend someone else's feast,
And my own sorrow.
And tell myself, from now on,
You possess the simple joy of a flower.

花語菩提

一

如果不被紅塵追趕
哪一朵花不是慈航普渡的佛
渡塵心　渡凡念　渡
人世載不動的清歡

花朵照亮的世界
不見君　不見民　唯見菩提佛心
庸人和雅客放下貪念
我　放下筆尖的執念

二

雪火流放的季節
漂流在渴慕中的天堂
無須日月輪流值守
那些水一樣趕路的花兒
那些芬芳的星子
將夢境　逐一點燃

我的童年躺在紙鳶上
紙鳶躺在花火裡
捨不得再飛向遠方

Flower Language and Bodhi

I

If not chased by the mortal dust
What flower is not a Buddha ferrying all beings across
Ferrying the dusty heart, ferrying mortal thoughts, ferrying
The pure joy the mortal world cannot bear

In the world lit by flowers
No lord is seen, no common folk, only the Bodhi Buddha's heart
The mediocre and the refined lay down their greed
I, lay down the obsession at the tip of my pen

II

In the season exiled by snow and fire
Drifting in a paradise of longing
No need for the sun and moon to stand guard in turn
Those flowers hurrying like water
Those fragrant stars
Light up the dreams, one by one

My childhood lies on a kite
The kite lies in the flower fire
Unwilling to fly far away again

三

煙花不是花
只把寂寞繡進夜色
當一場色彩繽紛的雪
葬了稻草人的影子
我凝視的目光
淌成含淚的河

花開　莊周的蝶夢將醒
花謝　梁祝的墓門已合
是花　總要熱烈開放一次
黯然凋零一生

四

暗夜如花　倒映水的寒光
思想的馬匹　披一路星花
絕塵而去　月亮若不轉身
我怎麼打馬回到前世

今夜　我蘸著瘦月清輝
畫一道溫暖的眼神
穿越暗夜裡的一盞燈花
赴來世月圓之約

III

Fireworks are not flowers
They only embroider loneliness into the night
When a colorful snow
Buries the scarecrow's shadow
My gazing eyes
Flow into a river of tears

When flowers bloom, Zhuang Zhou's butterfly dream
is about to wake
When flowers fade, the tomb gate of Liang Shanbo
and Zhu Yingtai has closed
To be a flower, one must bloom fervently once
And fade dimly for a lifetime

IV

The dark night is like a flower, reflecting the cold light of water
The steed of thought, draped in star flowers all the way
Gallops away without a trace. If the moon does not turn around
How can I ride back to my past life

Tonight, I dip my brush in the thin radiance of the moon
To paint a warm gaze
Passing through a spark of light in the dark night
To keep the appointment of the full moon in the next life

五

民間的花火姿態很低
聽嗩吶傾訴的幸福
心　總不免滲出淚花

別不相信　是卑微的螞蟻
用背收留了流浪的風
是幸福捉摸不定的含義
讓春天行色猶疑

甦醒的麻雀
試著抖去爪上泥痕
雲朵回暖
是時候　練習飛翔了

V

The folk flower fire holds its head low
Listening to the happiness poured out by the suona
The heart, inevitably, seeps out tears

Do not disbelieve—it is the humble ants
That shelter the wandering wind with their backs
It is the elusive meaning of happiness
That makes spring hesitate in its steps

The awakened sparrows
Try to shake off the mud from their claws
The clouds warm up
It is time to practice flying

南有喬木

南有喬木 或冰封的山巔 或蔭蔽的深谷 或若水的大道 或矯情的街巷
南有喬木 南方 因此被賦予靈性
　　　　　　　　　　　　　　　　——題記

南有喬木 喬木在山巔
冰雪淹沒剛直的身軀
從寬大的枝葉響過的鳥鳴
高一聲 低一聲
吹奏高原的神韻
吹奏離塵的天籟
上帝手指豎在雙唇間

南有喬木 喬木在深谷
飄零的落葉是遷徙的鳥群
隱藏于季節背後的精靈之舞
半是燦爛 半是靜穆
呈現生命相攜的指節
呈現輪回寂靜的過程
風 點燃季節的燈盞

南有喬木 喬木在大道
蔭萌似水 隨陽光月色流動
佇立的姿勢抒寫一諾千金
銘記生命的滄桑與真諦
飛揚的塵埃 人跡 車轍
執懷的隱者 沒有足跡地穿越
是對生命的禪悟

In the South, There Are Tall Trees

In the south, there are tall trees, Perhaps at the frozen mountaintop, Perhaps in the shadowed deep valley, Perhaps along the broad road like water, Or in the pretentious alleys, In the south, there are tall trees, Thus the south is endowed with spirit.—Epigraph

In the south, there are tall trees,
Tall trees at the mountaintop,
Ice and snow engulf their straightened forms.
From the wide branches, the calls of birds resound,
A high note, a low note, Playing the melody of the plateau,
Playing the celestial music that rises above the dust,
God's finger poised between his lips.

In the south, there are tall trees, Tall trees in the deep valley,
The falling leaves are migrating flocks of birds,
The dance of spirits hidden behind the seasons,
Half dazzling, half serene,
Displaying the interlinked joints of life,
Displaying the silent process of reincarnation,
The wind ignites the lamp of the seasons.

In the south, there are tall trees, Tall trees along the great road,
Shadows flowing like water, shifting with sunlight and moonlight,
Their standing posture writes a promise worth a thousand gold,
Remembering the vicissitudes and truths of life,
The soaring dust, the footprints of men, the wheel tracks,
The secluded hermit passes through without a trace,
A meditation on life.

南有喬木　喬木在街巷
相較於你的樸素　矯情的街巷
無法穿越你高遠曠達的上空
收攏和打開懷抱的瞬間
濾過的星光　讓守望的幸福
發出聲響　而你　始終就這樣
以純粹的孤獨　懸掛無根的欲念
塵世因此沒有傾斜

南有喬木　喬木在心裡
心靈的南方　水土適宜生長菩提
歲月在樹上開花掛果以後　我們可以
微傾了酒杯　淺啜一口紅塵
醉倒千年月色　和飲露的紅顏
一起歸隱地久天長

南有喬木　喬木一樣
與山相依為命的孩子們
在斧頭和油鋸砍伐沉默後的日子裡
該怎樣朗誦關於明天的幸福
讓我們的歸隱　沒有負罪和隱憂

南有喬木　心有菩提
啜泣的靈魂　該怎樣拷問斧頭和油鋸

In the south, there are tall trees, Tall trees in the alleys,
Compared to your simplicity, the pretentious alleys
Cannot transcend your lofty, vast sky,
In the moments when arms fold and unfold,
The starlight filtered through them makes the waiting happiness
Resonate, while you, always,
Hang desires with pure solitude,
Thus the dust of the world does not tilt.

In the south, there are tall trees, Tall trees in the heart,
The southern spirit of the soul, where the soil is right for the growth of bodhi,
After the years blossom and bear fruit on the tree, we may
Tilt our wine cups, gently sip the fleeting world,
Drunken under the moonlight of a thousand years,
And with the rosy faces drinking the dew,
Return to seclusion, lasting through the ages.

In the south, there are tall trees, Tall trees just the same,
Children who depend on the mountains,
In the days after the silence of the axe and the oil saw,
How should we recite the happiness of tomorrow?
Let our return to seclusion Be free from guilt and hidden worries.

In the south, there are tall trees, The heart holds bodhi,
How should the weeping soul interrogate the axe and the oil saw?

女皇 睡著的你還睜著眼嗎
——寫在廣元皇澤寺

今天是個節日 就因為你要換新妝
路上的人 就必須在暴雨中洗心革面

可包裹塵心的不止肉身
再大的暴雨 又怎能透穿
三尺紅塵堅硬的外殼

當我涉過泥濘 以佛子的虔誠
靜穆地肅立於你熟睡著的真容前
你 到底是三界外的佛
還是五蘊中的皇
端坐於塵世的引力之外
還那麼留戀那些漂浮的膝蓋嗎

曾經的女皇 我不曾叩首的陛下
今天 我就這樣站著和你對話
你也不用垂下尊嚴至上的頭

逝去太久的時光已經歸於未萌
遊走的光暈 在冷硬的石壁上
找不到落腳的巢

Empress, Are You Still Awake?

—*Written at Huangze Temple, Guangyuan*

Today is a festival, for you are to change your new adornment,
And the people on the road must wash their hearts in the torrential rain.

But what wraps the dusty heart is not just the flesh,
No matter how heavy the rain, how could it pierce
The hard shell of the three-foot world of dust?

When I wade through the mud with the sincerity of a Buddhist disciple,
I stand quietly before your sleeping form,
Are you the Buddha beyond the three realms,
Or the emperor within the five aggregates?
Seated outside the pull of this world,
Yet still longing for those floating knees?

Once a queen, I, who never bowed before you,
Today, I stand and converse with you,
You need not lower your head,
For your dignity is supreme.

The time that has long passed has returned to its beginning,
The wandering halos find no resting place on the cold, hard stone walls.

精疲力竭的龍脈 烏奴山 如今
被你隨意扯來 披作遮身的大氅
靈光隱遁以後 後世的目光
瘡孔斑駁

向佛的心靈還在喚你
蒙塵的靈魂還在喚你
可你的身體 早已不再是
安魂度心的回音壁

忠貞的嘉陵江 因你的誕生
從此 再沒合上過眼
就為作你的搖籃
你一個人的搖籃

曾經的女皇 我不曾叩首的陛下
我其實從不相信神話和傳說
只相信 你曾經的思想
怎樣深入一個時代的良心
在歷史的回流灣濺出金屬的聲響
任塵心的古井安詳地深入
佛土的彼岸

作為皇 你撫不平眾生的滄桑
作為佛 你撫不平世間的皺褶
可是 作為女人
你第一個和男人劃出平等的疆界
讓人與佛共存於一個靈魂

The weary dragon veins, Wunu Mountain,
Now casually draped by you as a cloak,
After the light retreats,
Future eyes fall upon it with scarred spots.

The heart of one who turns to Buddha still calls for you,
The soul, covered in dust, still calls for you,
But your body is no longer
The echo chamber that soothes souls and hearts.

The faithful Jialing River, since your birth,
Has never closed its eyes,
It became your cradle,
A cradle for you alone.

Once a queen, I, who never bowed before you,
I never truly believed in myths and legends,
But I believed in how your thoughts
Once penetrated the conscience of an era,
Making the sound of metal ripple in the flow of history,
While the ancient well of the dust-heart sinks calmly
Into the other shore of the Buddhist land.

As an empress, you could not smooth the sorrows of the people,
As a Buddha, you could not smooth the wrinkles of the world,
But as a woman,
You were the first to draw the boundary of equality with men,
Allowing humans and Buddha to coexist in one soul.

為此 我必須膜拜你
但不是以男人的膝
而是作為你後世的子民
以佇立的身體 彰顯出人與佛的比例
再以赤裸的目光走進你的傳奇
讓來自佛的消息
洗濯這帶罪之身

鳳凰南飛 回首北望
嘉陵江 是你北望時的淚光麼
你後世的女兒們 用你的淚花洗臉浴身
把利州這個古老的名字
輕靈地捧出浮世的煙塵之外

武則天 一個曾經把歷史攥在手裡
但歷史卻無法命名的女人
一個 夜明珠一樣鑲嵌在歷史的額際
需要閉上眼睛 才能感覺其光華的女人

一個 我無法從塵世的黑夜出發
探訪的女人……

For this, I must worship you,
But not with a man's knee,
Rather, as your descendants,
With my standing body, revealing the proportion of man and Buddha,
And with my naked gaze, walking into your legend,
Let the message from Buddha
Cleanse this sinful body.

The phoenix flies south, looking back to the north,
Is Jialing River the tear in your eyes as you look north?
Your daughters of the future, with your tears, wash their faces and bathe,
Gently lifting the ancient name of Lizhou
Out of the worldly dust.

Wu Zetian, a woman who once held history in her hands,
But history could not name her,
A woman like a night pearl, embedded in the forehead of history,
Whose radiance must be felt only when the eyes are closed.

A woman who I cannot leave the black night of this world to visit...

神話 陰謀與男兒美麗風骨（組詩）
——對話春秋男兒

一 勾踐 復仇是悲劇的開始

勾踐 如何想像
借一面文明的後視鏡 此刻
我與你狹路相逢在 2500 年以前

我看見 曾經罩在龍椅上的陰影
巨大得淹沒了你的存在
而你是內心有風暴的人 一旦迸發
吹皺的歷史 再也無法撫平

勾踐呵 如果沒有那個女人
以母性慈輝熄滅萬千重刀光劍影
鋪墊你距離王位的半步之遙
你如何在一念之間予取予求肝膽
可知身後 弱水氾濫
那美麗的魚化石遺世

彌留在大料上命懸遊絲地頓悟
無法跨越糧食和水的生命
只能在大愛神話裡復活
重生的你 於糞便中脫胎
於苦膽裡換骨

Myths, Conspiracy, and the Beauty of Manhood
— *A Dialogue with the Men of Spring and Autumn*

I. Goujian: Revenge as the Beginning of Tragedy

Goujian, how can we imagine?
Through the rearview mirror of civilization,
I now meet you on a narrow road, 2500 years ago.

I see the shadow once cast upon the dragon throne,
So vast it drowned out your very existence.
Yet you were a man of storms inside,
Once unleashed,
The ripples of history could never be smoothed.

Goujian, if not for that woman,
Who, with maternal warmth, extinguished the countless blades of fury,
Paving your way to within a step of the throne,
How would you, in the blink of an eye, offer your gall and liver?
Do you know behind you, the waters of Weakness flood?
That beautiful fish fossil, left behind by the world?

Lying on the great stone, life hanging by a thread,
Unable to cross over the grains and waters of life,
Only able to be reborn in the great myth of love,
Born again from filth,
Exchanged bones in bitter bile.

從悲劇出發　註定以悲劇結束
臥薪嚐膽的男人呵　不忍看你
立於枯骨中的悵茫與絕頂上的孤寂
在陽光拒絕鍍亮你的背影之前
女人永遠閉上了眼睛

勾踐呵　以城為墓的殯葬
是勝者為王的奢侈
還是俗世男兒深入骨髓的悲愴
這歲月冰逝已久的故事
流出新鮮的痛　化名愛情

Starting from tragedy, destined to end in tragedy,
The man who slept on brushwood and tasted gall,
I cannot bear to see you,
Standing amidst the withered bones, in melancholy and utter solitude,
Before the sun refuses to shine on your shadow,
The woman forever closed her eyes.

Goujian, the burial in the city's tomb,
Is it the luxury of the victor,
Or the sorrow deep within the bones of mortal men?
This tale, long frozen in time,
Spills fresh pain, now disguised as love.

二 夫差 並非紅顏禍水的理由

夫差 如果一直活到今天
你仍是萬千女人爭寵的男兒
只是當初 隨你征戰的駿馬
已經無法褪去滿身血跡 還原潔白

庶出 你血氣裡噴薄的雄心霸氣
封凍在皇宮森冷重帷裡
骨子裡正直與善良的秉性
正好驅趕著你 靠近民間

獨不該在那一刻揮劍呵
出逃悲劇真相的弱女子
懼怕的已不再是霜刃冷芒
而是淪陷權欲深淵的心靈
這世間最大的黑暗

夫差 縱橫三千里血河的男兒
卻逃不出女人用生命寫下的咒
當你迷醉蹈火仇恨烈焰的快感時
你雙腳踏住的不是天下
而是謊言粉飾的地獄之門

戰火憔悴了土地 鐵蹄踏瘦了民間
五穀拒絕了炊煙 女人背叛了愛情
夫差呵 當你以王的名義
肆意穿越女人身體的極樂
誰看見你繞道心靈的酸楚

II. Fuchai: Not the Reason for the Femme Fatale

Fuchai, if you lived until today,
You would still be the man sought after by thousands of women,
But back then, the warhorses that fought by your side
Could never remove the bloodstains, returning them to purity.

Born of a concubine, your boundless ambition and domineering spirit,
Frozen in the cold, heavy palace curtains,
The righteous and kind nature within you,
Drove you closer to the people.

But you should not have raised your sword then,
Against the weak woman fleeing the truth of tragedy,
What she feared was no longer the cold gleam of the sword,
But the abyss of desires for power,
The greatest darkness in the world.

Fuchai, a man who crossed three thousand miles of blood rivers,
Yet could not escape the curse written by a woman's life,
When you reveled in the fiery pleasure of hate,
What you stood upon was not the world,
But the door to a hell disguised by lies.

War withered the land, iron hooves starved the people,
Grains rejected the cooking smoke, women betrayed love,
Fuchai, when you, in the name of a king,
Ravaged a woman's body in your bliss,
Who saw the bitterness you skirted in your heart?

終是那最後飲恨一抹
止息紅顏禍水　傾城也好
傾國也罷　不過以疤痕的淒美
裝點歷史本已輝煌的典籍

與你僅相隔一頁　我卻只能
眼睜睜看你把悲劇演繹徹底
為此　我當於靈魂之上置杯
盛男兒的血也盛男兒的淚

當我提前痛飲了自己無法終結的悲劇
夫差　請打馬從我的文字裡
回到生長五穀的民間
我陪著你一起放牧
煙火中生生不息的愛情

In the end, that final, regretful moment,
Stops the femme fatale, whether it be a city or a nation,
But merely adorns the already glorious history
With the mournful beauty of scars.

Only one page separates us, yet I can only
Watch as you completely play out the tragedy,
For this, I shall place a cup above my soul,
To hold the blood of men and the tears of men.

When I drink the tragedy that I cannot end,
Fuchai, please ride away from my words,
Back to the people who grow the grains,
I will accompany you to pasture,
The everlasting love born in fireworks.

三 範蠡 男兒的美麗風骨

從你身上 我看見放浪形骸
是一個男人多大的智慧
置身杯中 飲醉孤獨之後
頭枕一泓潔白的亂世清夢

而你終究是受命之人
註定要將風華融會潮漲潮落的歷史
並最終以光芒的名義
寫就男兒傳奇的經典

當愛情屬每個角落的時候
你孤獨的心靈卻遭受著風雪
命運沒收了你所有退路
逼你拔劍 謀一代民生未來

戰爭背景下越是美麗的的女人
就越可能成為最鋒利的武器
當你以無極的智慧拒絕了愛情
也就拒絕了最致命的傷害

於是你孤注一擲 赴湯蹈火
於是你運籌帷幄 決勝千里
洞悉了霸業光環裡暗藏的殺機
你決然抽身於功成名就之時

III. Fan Li: The Beauty of Manhood

From you, I see how one can live unrestrained,
What great wisdom lies within a man's release,
After drunkenly embracing the solitude,
Resting my head upon the clear, white chaos of a dream.

Yet, in the end, you are the one chosen by fate,
Destined to weave the elegance of rising tides and falling history,
And finally, in the name of brilliance,
Write the classic legend of manhood.

When love belongs to every corner,
Your lonely heart is still weathered by storms,
Fate has taken away all your retreat,
Forcing you to draw your sword,
To secure the future of the people.

In the context of war, the more beautiful the woman,
The sharper the weapon she may become,
When you, with boundless wisdom, reject love,
You also reject the most lethal wound.

Thus, you gamble it all, stepping into fire,
You strategize, conquering across thousands of miles,
Seeing through the hidden assassinations in the halo of dominion,
And decisively withdraw at the height of your success.

作為飲者　你揮灑酒至微醺的淋漓
作為男人　你寫意花看半開的妙境
作為卿相　你彰顯臨頂抽身的瀟灑
作為布衣　你演繹濟世儒商的品節

復仇男人揮劍擊穿　以及
到下王者血染的歷史早已結痂
史冊因你歸隱而空缺的一頁
而今　擁擠著拜謁的心靈

我當以我的方式記住了你　範蠡
我們不說功名　不說愛情　不說恩仇
說一個男兒的美麗風骨
是怎樣傾倒了時空

As a drinker, you lavish the wine, slightly intoxicated,
As a man, you paint the subtle beauty of half-opened flowers,
As a prime minister, you demonstrate the elegant detachment of withdrawal,
As a commoner, you portray the integrity of a merchant who aids the world.

The vengeful man raises his sword to pierce,
And the history stained with the blood of kings has already scabbed over.
The page left empty by your retreat from history,
Now crowded with the souls that come to pay homage.

I will remember you in my own way, Fan Li,
We speak not of fame, nor love, nor grudges,
But of the beauty of manhood,
And how it topples the very fabric of time and space.

桃花,或生命意象

一

當我寫下桃花 心空便有了繽紛
牌坊山 歇足的神自高處
撒落的花瓣 淌滿茶堡河
河邊梳妝後出嫁的母親
用河水餵養我 我的胎記
長成一枚桃花

二

以鳥的姿態學習飛翔
茶堡河 照見我翅膀上的絨毛
大山深處的春天 只一聲喊山的號子
就羞紅了臉 我看見的白
是桃花惟一的原色

仍有更高處的凝視
將我釘在塵世 入土三分

Peach Blossoms, or the Symbolism of Life

I

When I write "peach blossoms,"
My heart fills with colors and vibrance.
At the Paifang Mountain,
The resting gods from the heights
Scatter petals,
Filling the Tea Fortress River.
A mother, who after her grooming, leaves for marriage by the river,
Feeds me with the river water,
And my birthmark grows into a peach blossom.

II

I learn to fly,
Imitating the bird's posture.
The Tea Fortress River reflects the down on my wings.
In the depths of the great mountain's spring,
A single shout echoes,
And the mountain blushes.
The white I see is the only original color of peach blossoms.

Still, there is a gaze from a higher place,
Nailing me to the dust of the world,
Burying me three parts deep.

三

如果天空是我死後的鏡子
一抔黃土　就是我永不凋謝的愛情
就讓我以桃花的名義
預約一季璀璨
不必來世

四

桃花故里　花海如潮
輕浮的目光像蔽日的浮雲
都是些看不見幸福花瓣呵
結出的果　被誰的嘴品啞甘甜

我不是賞花的人
只是每到這樣的季節
我身體裡的胎記總是隱隱作疼
仿佛一轉身　那些繽紛的桃花
就會一路凋零在我的背影裡

III

If the sky is the mirror after my death,
Then a handful of yellow earth
Is my everlasting love.
Let me, in the name of peach blossoms,
Pre-book a season of brilliance.
No need for another life.

IV

In the homeland of peach blossoms,
The sea of flowers surges like waves.
Light, fleeting gazes like clouds hiding the sun,
Yet none can see the happiness of petals.
Who will taste the sweetness of the fruit it bears?

I am not the one who appreciates flowers.
But every time this season comes,
The birthmark inside me aches faintly,
As though, with a turn of the head,
Those colorful peach blossoms
Will wilt in the shadow of my back.

五

入眼的花瓣　肆意割傷我的目光
嫣紅或梨白　那不是桃花的顏色
是我眼裡滴出的血

當我伸出感恩的手　自塵緣的玄關
寫你的另一種魂魄
有風　笑得很輕浮

六

既然開在了塵世　桃花
你怎能抗拒物語的手
暴虐地擦傷離我們最近的星空
從桃花出發　我們真的就能
回到愛情

我已經是自己背影的囚徒
原諒我　無法葬盡落花

V

The petals that meet my eyes,
Cut into my gaze. Crimson or pearly white,
These are not the colors of peach blossoms.
They are the blood that drips from my eyes.

When I stretch out a grateful hand from the threshold of fate,
I write another version of your soul.
The wind laughs lightly,
As though it were frivolous.

VI

Since you bloom in the world, peach blossoms,
How can you resist the hand of story?
Ruthlessly, it scratches the starry sky closest to us.
From peach blossoms, can we really return to love?

I have already become a prisoner of my own shadow,
Forgive me,
I cannot bury the fallen flowers.

七

如果可以選擇
我又怎敢命犯桃花
前世種下的毒
沒有任何徵兆地發作
清明又至

閃滅的輪迴中　桃花
一旦落塵　你怎麼守住
冰清玉潔的原身

VII

If I could choose,
How dare I let myself be cursed by the peach blossoms?
The poison sown in my past life,
Suddenly erupts without warning.
Clear and bright, Qingming arrives.

In the flashing cycles of reincarnation, peach blossoms,
Once they fall to the dust,
How can you preserve
Your pure and flawless original form?

雨中靜坐

一

雨　也是一種淚
和神靈的喜怒無關
玻璃　把我們安放於時光的背面
感恩抑或救贖的念頭
讓我們有了雨滴的輕靈與自由
於是　我們穿越與抵達的速度
正好與天堂塵世的距離吻合

二

這樣的雨日　陷落紅塵的我們
是不是可以　心凝成湖
在流星劃過夜的明眸時
借此　也為藏身蓮棚下的前世愛情
點上來世的朱紅

經過一座風雨橋
我們從容經過前生來世
憑一聲鳥鳴的牽引

Sitting Still in the Rain

I

Rain is also a kind of tear,
Unrelated to the joy or anger of the gods.
The glass places us on the other side of time,
With thoughts of gratitude or redemption,
We gain the lightness and freedom of raindrops.
Thus, our speed of crossing and arriving
Matches the distance between heaven and earth.

II

On such rainy days, we, fallen into the mortal world,
Can we not condense our hearts into a lake?
When the meteor cuts across the night's bright eyes,
Can we also light up the next life's vermilion
For the love that hides under the lotus canopy of past lives?

Passing through a wind and rain bridge,
We calmly pass between past and future lives,
Guided by a bird's song.

三

雨中　亮起的風景　舞著長長的水袖
旋動生活的靜水　閉上眼睛
想像一次虹降　打開蜿蜒的四季
永浴春光的心靈　呼吸間完成的預言
讓夢想的白馬越過早上的太陽
與日落的家園　殊途同歸

睜開眼睛的時候　睫毛上的雨
正好滴落花開的內心

四

雨　幽遠的意境裡
雪是一種透明的陰影
靜坐雨中　如一粒忘卻疼痛的雪
收藏了太陽的芳心　雨落的過程
有火的痕跡　一如此刻的我
以一種如水的心緒
點亮自己

III

In the rain, the scenery lit up dances with long water sleeves,
Spinning the still waters of life.
Close your eyes,
Imagine a rainbow descending,
Opening the winding seasons,
A spirit bathed forever in springtime light,
A prophecy fulfilled with every breath.
Let the white horse of dreams cross the morning sun,
And reach the sunset home,
Both paths leading to the same end.

When you open your eyes, the rain on your lashes
Perfectly falls into the blooming heart.

IV

Rain, in its distant symbolism,
Snow is a transparent shadow.
Sitting quietly in the rain, like a snowflake that has forgotten pain,
I have stored the heart of the sun.
The process of rain falling
Bears the traces of fire,
Just like this moment,
Where, with a watery heart,
I illuminate myself.

五

花朵點燈；凜凜涼意
恍如靈魂的質地　此刻
最適宜向陳釀借一種品質
在掌心泊一些陽光
將自己的影子孕化成匙
如水時刻　醉或醒開啟的將是
同一鎖孔
此刻　用靈魂大聲喊出的動詞　淨
與身處的境遇無關

六

天上有燈　地上有星
一張唇吻亮另一張唇
飲雨的塵世呵　怎能沒有愛
花蕊包裹的秘密
麥芒銜走的往事
一年四季　都有雨的情書
往返不同的時空
安坐雨中　就用藍色的眼睛
看看生活缺口裡的風景
或在一封情書裡
化一尾會飛的魚

V

Flowers light up,
A coolness in the air,
As if the texture of the soul,
This moment,
The best time to borrow a quality from aged wine.
Hold some sunlight in the palm,
Transform my shadow into a key.
In the moment of water,
Drunk or sober, we open the same lock.
In this moment,
The verb shouted by the soul is purity,
Unrelated to the circumstances we are in.

VI

There are lights in the sky, stars on the ground,
One lip kisses the other.
In the dusty world, how can there be no love?
The secret wrapped in flower petals,
The past carried by the wheat stalks,
Every season, there are love letters in the rain,
Traveling through different time and space.
Sitting still in the rain,
With blue eyes,
Look at the scenery in the gaps of life.
Or, in a love letter,
Transform into a fish that can fly.

七

誰會記住一場雨 記住
那些曾經母性的光輝
恍如佛在高處撒落的念珠
敲打塵世的煙火
面對恩澤的雨 我只想枕樽而眠
我知道 流亡在文字蒙難的路上
給我溫暖的 註定是另一場
下給靈魂的火焰雨

八

能化身一滴雨嗎
穿越文字森嚴的方陣
揮手成最後的結句 儘管落寞
儘管生命之杯由此傾斜
然塵世的歸路已然清晰
生命的玄關已然洞開

就以燃燭舔香的素手 舉杯
萬千紅塵 我只啜一小口
便能醉了千年月色

VII

Who will remember a rainstorm, remember
The maternal brilliance once given?
Like beads dropped by the Buddha from above,
Striking the fireworks of the world.
In the face of the rain of blessings,
I only wish to sleep with a wine jug as my pillow.
I know, exiled on the road where words suffer,
The one who warms me is destined to be another rain,
A fire-rain falling upon my soul.

VIII

Can I transform into a raindrop?
Crossing the forest of words,
Waving my hand to form the final sentence,
Even if loneliness lingers,
Even if the cup of life tilts from here,
The way back to the mortal world is already clear.
The threshold of life is already open.

With a hand that lights candles and licks the fragrance,
I raise my cup,
In this vast world of dust, I only sip a small mouthful,
And am intoxicated by the moonlight of a thousand years.

九

雨日放歌
誰的雙眸飽蘸生活的底蘊
竹的清韻　梅的冷品
桃花的豔　海棠的媚

不去說蓮吧
睡在唐風宋韻中的那點心事
經不起風塵中的一點俗念

且飲雨　自會心香流轉
尋我　已在塵外

IX

Singing in the rain,
Whose eyes are soaked in the essence of life?
The pure sound of bamboo, the cold temperament of plum,
The beauty of peach blossoms, the charm of begonia,

We won't speak of the lotus,
Resting in the Tang wind and Song rhythm,
That delicate thought,
Unable to withstand a single mundane notion.

So let us drink the rain,
The heart's fragrance will naturally flow,
Seek me, I am already beyond the dust.

紙樣年華

一 白晝 詩人的苦難

上帝睜開眼睛 我們便看見了光
作為黑夜的覺醒者 詩人
在白晝看見的是夜的另一種呈現
譬如 自己的眼睛和一切影像的陰影

最大的苦難 來自心靈的夜色
讓詩人習慣用眼光去捕捉生活的褶皺
把抖落的時間碎片當成精神的花瓣
失真的世界 盲者的抽象
詩人因此痛苦不堪

被黑夜賦予黑色眼睛的詩人
最終清醒地選擇走入永寂的暗夜
把帶不走的身影 留給白晝
證明 陰影也是一種光

所以詩人 形骸作馬 精神為鳥
奔跑的宿命 飛升的涅磐
所有移植的夢想 都在一張紙上完成
而塵世的符咒和來自神的諭示

The Paper-like Years

I. The Day: The Poet's Suffering

When God opens His eyes, we see the light.
As the awakener of the night, the poet
Sees in the day another form of night.
For example, the shadow of their own eyes and all images.

The greatest suffering comes from the darkness of the soul,
Which forces the poet to capture the wrinkles of life with their gaze,
Turning the scattered fragments of time into petals of the spirit.
The distorted world, the abstract of the blind,
And thus, the poet suffers unbearably.

Gifted with black eyes by the night,
The poet ultimately chooses to walk into the eternal silence of darkness,
Leaving behind the image they cannot carry,
To prove that shadows are also a form of light.

So, the poet, body as horse, spirit as bird,
Chasing their inevitable fate, ascending in Nirvana.
All transplanted dreams are completed on a single sheet of paper,
Yet the earthly spells and divine decrees

都無力穿透靈魂的子午線
所以 其實脆弱
是一種詩人先天的基因

陽光總是讓詩人靈魂出竅
月光總是悲情的化身
晨露是一種淚水
晚霞的色彩沒有溫度
而這一切 與白晝有關
與詩人的苦難有關

白晝 詩人在幻化的物象中
治療中毒的神經和靈魂
象一隻永遠走不出黑夜的蟋蟀
不在上帝的上眼皮
就在下眼皮

Are powerless to penetrate the meridian of the soul.
Therefore, fragility
Is an inherent gene of the poet.

Sunlight always draws the poet's soul out of their body,
Moonlight always embodies sorrow,
Morning dew is a form of tears,
And the colors of the sunset are void of warmth.
And all of this is related to the day,
And to the poet's suffering.

In the day, the poet, amidst the shifting symbols of things,
Heals the poisoned nerves and soul,
Like a cricket that will never escape the night,
Not on God's upper eyelid,
But on the lower eyelid.

二 黑夜 詩人脫掉的外衣

燈光 是白晝對黑夜滲透的方式
無數的廓門打開 這時候
詩人的目光看得很遠 直抵
夢的源頭 那黑色的背靜

然而 燈是無法把黑夜燃盡的
匍匐於燈下的背影
在詩人脫掉外衣以後
還是沒有減少黑的厚度
一如 黑夜無法在一張紙上
著墨

能讓身體透明起來的 惟夢鄉
當詩人捂滅內心的燈盞
沿月光與夢境交錯的方向
踏入靈魂的門檻 和自己的落日
安然相對

這時候 沒有痛楚從呼吸裡擠出
適合完成一些溫情的詩篇
譬如愛情 即使城堡的大門緊閉
只是簡單的經過 就足以讓詩人
把顫慄的心緒保持到天明

II. The Night: The Poet's Shed Skin

Light is the way daylight permeates the night.
Countless archways open, and at this moment,
The poet's gaze reaches far, straight to
The source of dreams, the quiet blackness.

However, light cannot burn away the night.
The shadow crawling beneath the light,
Even after the poet sheds their outer garments,
Does not diminish the thickness of the darkness.
Just as the night cannot be written
On a sheet of paper.

What makes the body transparent is only the dreamland.
When the poet extinguishes the light in their heart,
Following the moonlight and the winding path of dreams,
They step onto the threshold of the soul,
Meeting their own sunset calmly.

At this moment, no pain is squeezed out of the breath,
It is the perfect time to finish some warm poems,
Such as love. Even if the castle gates are tightly closed,
A simple passing is enough for the poet
To keep their trembling heart until dawn.

活在這樣一個紙質的年代
沒有英雄　只有詩人
縛身在薄紙厚繭中　如蛹的詩人
怎能不渴望在一次愛情的巨大催化中
破繭化蝶　把這些無休無止的黑夜
舉重若輕

鋪夜幕為紙　鋪夢鄉為紙
讓生命中必經的雨滴和雪花
坦然地降臨　沐浴詩人疲累的軀體
讓淨光在上帝閉上眼睛以前
進駐詩人的心靈
讓閃電　昭示一個詩人
真實的靈魂

Living in such a paper-like age,
There are no heroes, only poets,
Bound in thin paper and thick calluses, like a cocoon.
How can the poet not long to break free from this shell
In a great catalytic moment of love,
To emerge as a butterfly,

Lifting the endless nights, With effortless grace?
Spread the night sky as paper, spread the dreamland as paper,
Let the rain and snow,
Which must fall in life,
Come gently, bathing the poet's weary body.
Let the pure light enter the poet's soul
Before God closes His eyes,
And let the lightning reveal
The poet's true soul.

天堂裡　每顆星星都是鳴唱的蟋蟀

——緬懷流沙河先生

此站陽關　不復明日
先生此去　天堂就此眉目清晰
不過是另一維度美好之所在
從此　每一顆星星都是鳴唱的蟋蟀

在這樣一個行色猶疑的冬天
停止生長的思想裝滿彈藥
保持緘默的嘴唇隱入辭說
我們當以食指豎唇劃清與曖昧的界限

以先生之清臞　實在不必
負重一個時代的良知遠行
所有從流沙盡頭醒來的文字
必定如經樂的溫暖深入熟寐的安詳

打開是理想之光　合上如白魚之棲
當臺北的鄉愁飲露而來
先生的蟋蟀唱響一代人的夏天
更唱響詩歌的火熱盛世
從一滴清涼鳥鳴喚醒的山村出發
我便是那理想比衣衫單薄的小少年

In Heaven, Every Star is a Cricket Singing

— *In Memory of Mr. Liu Shaha*

This station is Yangguan, no tomorrow to return.
Once you depart, sir, Heaven will finally have its clear outline.
It's just another dimension of beauty,
From now on, every star will be a cricket singing.

On such a winter day, hesitant and drifting,
The thoughts that cease to grow are filled with ammunition.
Silent lips withdraw into words,
And we must use our index finger to draw a line,
To separate us from the ambiguity.

With your purity, sir, there is no need
To carry the burden of an era's conscience on your long journey.
All the words that wake up from the end of the flowing sands
Will surely dive into the warmth of hymns,
Deep into the tranquil peace of sleep.

Open, and there is the light of ideals.
Close, like the white fish's resting place.
When Taipei's nostalgia drinks the morning dew,
Your crickets sing the summer of a generation,
And sing the fiery golden age of poetry.
From the mountain village awakened by the call of a single cool bird,
I am the thin boy whose ideals are frailer than his clothes.

膜拜與朝覲　禦寒與卸重　詩歌於我
是另一種呼吸　另一種活著

先生的薦語　更像是一道符咒
將我封印在文字的美妙歧途
我全力以赴想要抵達的終點
不過是比生命本身更大的空和荒

一如此刻　當文字成為思想的流體
我卻不在岸上　也沒有渡船
甚至不能成為流體的一部分
這生不瞑目的痛　卻日復一日

既然做不了不食周粟的鳥
索性做回吞咽麥芒的凡夫
好在有星光的夜晚　飽食之後
還可以靜聽　來自天堂　蟋蟀的鳴唱

Worship and pilgrimage, warmth and release,
Poetry to me is another kind of breath, another kind of life.

Your words, sir, are like a spell,
Sealing me into the wonderful detours of words.
The endpoint I strive to reach
Is but a greater emptiness and desolation
Than life itself.

Just like now,
When words become the fluid of thoughts,
But I am not on the shore, nor is there a boat.
I can't even become a part of the fluid.
This pain, which will not allow me to rest in peace,
But endures, day after day.

Since I can't be the bird that does not eat the grains of Zhou,
I might as well be the common man who swallows the awn of wheat.
Fortunately, on starry nights, after I am full,
I can still listen in silence,
To the cricket song from Heaven.

麗水金沙之柔軟時光

一

在接近的想像中
我病情加重
他們說　麗江
是都市人的藥

我仍全副武裝　以此防備
傳說的不可靠

二

十點的夜色　溫軟如水
適合莫名的感傷
像落滿歎息的小河一樣靜淌

凝固的天籟　我們
最後的天籟

Soft Time of Lishui Golden Sands

I

In the approaching imagination,
My condition worsens.
They say Lijiang
Is the medicine for city people.

Yet I remain fully armored,
Guarding against the unreliable legends.

II

The night at ten is soft as water,
Perfect for inexplicable sorrow,
Like a river full of sighs, flowing quietly.

The frozen symphony, we
The final symphony.

三

土陶居　河燈一樣
漂在時光古典的意境裡
鄉音　被誰截竹為笛橫在嘴邊
都是神遊的人呵
甘願　和這遍地古跡
一起隱姓埋名

從白族古老的民居醒來
從八百年的幽夢中醒來
數聲清亮的鳥鳴
霧濕了身心

四

石砌的街道　時間的斷面
腳印沉下去　如魚在水
滿目光潤的凹凸曲線
食色的歷史　茹毛飲血

飄在古城　不論哪個方向
都有最柔軟的心意
伴隨迷路的幸福
忘了自己的所在
忘了腳下的路
隨意飄著　飄著
佛子一般

III

In the earthen houses, the river lights drift,
Like lanterns on the timeless shores of time.
The village sound—
Who has carved bamboo into a flute by their lips?
These are the souls who roam,
Willing to vanish,
Along with the ancient relics.

Waking up from the ancient Bai houses,
Waking from eight hundred years of dreams,
A few sharp bird calls,
Mist covering body and soul.

IV

The stone-paved streets are the cross-sections of time,
Footprints sinking, like fish in water.
The curves and dips bathe in light,
The history of eating raw, drinking blood.

Drifting in the ancient town,
No matter which direction,
There is the softest heart,
Accompanying the happiness of getting lost.
Forgetting where we are,
Forgetting the road beneath our feet,
Floating, floating,
Like a child of Buddha.

五

酒吧　孤旅的驛站
像老朋友一樣　與自己對坐
在情感的回流灣
泊一些柔軟的情節

並與金屬包裹的內心
相持　最終握手言和

一個人的豔遇
一個人的上帝

六

在古城
每一塊石磚都在呼吸
每一絲空氣都在訴說
悠然的語氣　與我們
相隔久遠年代

腳步儘量放慢　再慢
呼吸儘量放緩　再緩
在一個不期的閃念中
與自己　恍若隔世

V

The bar is the inn for the lonely traveler,
Like an old friend, sitting across from myself,
In the bay of emotional reflection,
I park some soft stories.

And with the metal-clad heart,
We hold each other in a quiet truce.

A solitary romantic encounter,
A solitary God.

VI

In the ancient town,
Every stone brick breathes,
Every breath of air tells a story,
A leisurely tone, connecting us
To a distant era.

Step slowly, even slower,
Breathe slowly, even slower,
In an unexpected flash,
I am as if from another world.

七

對一個外籍老人的敬仰
我選擇　遠遠地矚望
想像一場威力無匹的颶風
掀起覆雪的金頂
讓老人的靈覺
繼續飛揚

可老人睡了
在雪之下　在塵之上
玉龍雪山　是他的夢塚

八

天上的街市　沒有人來人往
他們都下凡了

古城的燈火亮一盞
天上的星星就掉一顆
雨　越下越大

漲水的銀河　放河燈的人群裡
沒有神仙的影子
時間的目的地　不分此岸和彼岸
凡人的相思就不會拐彎

VII

In admiration of an elderly foreigner,
I choose to watch from afar,
Imagining a mighty hurricane,
Lifting the snow-covered golden peak,
Letting the old man's spiritual perception
Continue to soar.

But the old man sleeps,
Beneath the snow, above the dust.
Yulong Snow Mountain is his tomb of dreams.

VIII

In the heavenly market, no one comes or goes,
They have all descended to the mortal realm.

When the ancient town's lamps are lit,
A star from the sky falls.
The rain grows heavier,

The rising river of the Milky Way, in the crowds releasing lanterns,
There is no trace of immortals.
The destination of time knows no boundaries
Between this shore and the other shore,
The yearning of mortals does not turn corners.

九

琳琅滿目的店鋪　像盛裝的情人
來的都是有緣人嗎

精品　絕品　極品
何必慧眼　但為心儀
除去濃墨重彩的包裹
最大的贗品是我們自己

讓塗脂抹粉的靈魂
見上帝去吧

十

老得只剩下睡眠的納西古樂
鬍鬚伸入隔世的東巴經
塵世的腳步　止於
古老傳奇的門檻

去了麗江　回來的不是玄奘
不去麗江　我們依然是
活在自己的神話裡
五行山下的大聖

紅塵很硬　麗江很軟
容不得久駐

IX

The dazzling shops, like lovers in festive attire,
Do the destined ones come?

High-quality, exquisite, top-notch.
Why search for a keen eye when the heart already yearns?
Remove the heavy wrapping of bright colors,
The greatest counterfeit is ourselves.

Let the souls painted in rouge
Go meet God.

X

The Naxi ancient music, now only sleep remains,
Beard stretching into the otherworldly Dongba scriptures,
The steps of the world halt
At the threshold of ancient legends.

Going to Lijiang, the one who returns is not Xuanzang.
Not going to Lijiang, we are still
Living in our own myth,
The great sage beneath the Five Elements Mountain.

The red dust is hard, Lijiang is soft,
Not suitable for long stays.

邊緣隱居劄記（一組）

一 遁

我是風塵布衣 我這麼認為的時候
一個姓易的傢夥死得不明不白
彌留時 最後一縷光的詩意 風的經典
成了他無法瞑目的痛

其實以我之俗 連一件裹身的布衣
也是無根妄念地編撰以及骨骸地捐付
拋卻詩意 從我頭頂肆虐盜走光陰的手
並不黑 反呈魔幻般的媚惑

肩部以上下顎以下隱藏的生死分界線
脆弱的不是血光地輕易迸濺
而是懸而未落 時光鋒刃地威逼
我密匝的鬍鬚 只用來隱藏觸世的韌性
而非引頸就戮生存堅硬哲學的真相

你們說起的風塵布衣
是我提前轉世的靈魂
骷髏一樣決絕無畏地行走
我只想證明 一切活著的疼痛
並非源於華麗的世襲

Edge Dweller's Journal (A Series)

I: Escape

I am the common man of the dust and dirt.
When I think this, a fellow named Yi dies without explanation.
In his dying moments, the final streak of light, the poetry of wind,
Becomes the pain he cannot forget.

In truth, with my mundane nature,
Even a piece of cloth that covers my body
Is a product of rootless delusion, a gift of bones.
I abandon poetry, as the hands that steal time
Are not black, but seductively magical.

The boundary between life and death hides above my shoulders, beneath my jaw,
The fragility lies not in the blood easily spilled,
But in the threatening, hovering passage of time.
My thick beard only serves to hide the resilience that touches the world,
Not to make my neck an offering to the harsh truths of survival.

You speak of the man in the dust,
He is the spirit of my former life,
Walking resolutely, like a skeleton,
I only want to prove that all living pain
Does not stem from noble inheritance.

二 溫暖

光陰多像是樽精美的水晶棺
我靜靜躺在裡面
看身外落葉飄零的世界

記取了陽光的味道　落葉安詳
記取了光陰的味道　我也安詳

我安詳地堅持著用寫字的方式
在生命裡鑽木取火
等待光陰斂葬
我馨香的骨殖

知道大地始終溫暖如惜
我已不在意　生命
在某一刻　停歇

II: Warmth

Time is much like a beautifully crafted crystal coffin.
I lie quietly inside,
Watching the world outside as leaves fall, drifting away.

I remember the taste of sunlight, the serenity of fallen leaves,
I remember the taste of time, and I too remain serene.

I remain serene, insisting on writing,
Using my words to kindle fire in life,
Waiting for time to gather in my fragrant bones.

Knowing that the earth is always warm and tender,
I no longer mind when life pauses
At some unmarked moment.

三 毒藥

靈魂有痛的人
在黑夜裡比白晝更容易
獲取溫暖

一如此刻 我無限放大的瞳孔
將黑夜逼視成一隻渺小的螞蟻
卻被一枚無知無畏的時針
定格成抹殺不掉的罪證

靈魂是個怎樣的巫師
總是用毒藥來拯救活著的人
譬如陰謀 譬如黑暗
譬如欲望

III: Poison

The soul in pain
Is more easily warmed in the night than in the day.
Like now, my infinitely magnified pupils

Stare into the night, shrinking it to a tiny ant,
Only to be fixed by an ignorant, fearless clock hand,
An indelible proof of guilt.

What kind of sorcerer is the soul?
It always uses poison to save the living,
Like conspiracy, like darkness,
Like desire.

四 雅裡的天堂

此刻 我是趕赴你音樂裡春天的蝴蝶
此刻 我是繾綣你藍色愛情裡的王子
此刻 音樂若水 大道若水
此刻 我是你天堂裡的雲

一季花開 一場雪融 一次輪回
只在兩個音符之間
此曲與彼曲之間 那瑰麗流淌的旋律
就是我迷離的前世和明媚的今生嗎

雅裡 你燦爛的音樂其實是宿命的極至
死在一次聆聽之後的是人
永生的是善愛的心

當紅塵在你的音樂裡化為柔軟的一泓
我只想做那不落塵的一片輕羽
永遠追隨 無限靠近
但決不忘情地陷身

往返在塵世與你的天堂之間的路上
我一直沒敢忘記腳下的剎車板

IV: Heaven in Elegance

At this moment, I am the butterfly heading to the spring in your music,
At this moment, I am the prince entwined in your blue love,
At this moment, music is like water, the great way is like water,
At this moment, I am the cloud in your heaven.

A season's bloom, a snowfall's melt, a cycle reborn,
All between two notes,
Between this melody and that,
The flowing beauty of the melody,
Is it my hazy past life or my bright present life?

In elegance, your splendid music is indeed the pinnacle of fate.
The person who dies after one listen is human,
The one who lives forever is the heart full of good love.

When the dust becomes a soft pool in your music,
I only want to be that light feather,
Forever following, infinitely approaching,
But never falling deeply into it.

On the road between the world and your heaven,
I have never dared to forget the brake beneath my feet.

五 敬畏

是衣物讓我們成為恒溫動物
是糧食救贖了我們作為人的尊嚴

一粒石頭穿著自己的衣服 很乾淨
一枚草葉吃著自己的糧食 很乾淨
我們也很乾淨 因為衣物和糧食

緘默的日子 我總看見黑夜的土地上
許多勞作的人影
仿佛無數化身的我

他們種植另一種糧食用來辟穀
紡織另一種衣物用來隱形
他們想證明一種乾淨
無關人的原罪

只是我曾經寫下的文字
早已成為今生脫不掉的囚衣
此後 我的緘默
惟因敬畏

V: Reverence

It is clothing that makes us warm-blooded animals,
It is food that redeems our dignity as humans.

A stone, clothed in its own skin, is clean,
A grass blade, feeding on its own sustenance, is clean,
We are clean, because of our clothing and food.

In the silent days, I often see shadows of laborers
On the land of the black night,
Like countless incarnations of myself.

They plant another kind of food to stave off hunger,
They weave another kind of clothing to become invisible,
They seek to prove a purity,
Unrelated to human original sin.

But the words I once wrote
Have long become the prison garments of this life,
Since then, my silence
Has been nothing but reverence.

金沙，再次鍍亮的不是光芒（組詩）

一 遺址

最先找到你的 不是人類
更不是那枚帶著神諭的古香果樹葉
是那些走錯路 覓食的螻蟻
偷吃了埋在地下 神話的果實

而此刻 時光的細節成為盈握在手的沙
那些捧在考古學家手裡的金
冷漠 不是因為失憶
是離開愛情太久

多矯情啊 掃帚掃去的兩公分
竟然是一方天空新的高度
你是蜀人麼 那麼你的榮耀
已經三千年

我是蜀人 可我是葬在陽光裡的人
詩歌是我的遺址
而那些把自己葬在土壤裡的先人們
金沙是你們的遺址

我並不冀望後人從我的遺址裡找到我
就象我不願意從你們的遺址
遭遇和金一樣柔軟的愛情

"Golden Sands, Not Radiance But Another Polished Truth" (A Series of Poems)

I: Relics

The first to find you were not humans,
Nor the ancient fruit leaves carrying divine oracles,
But those ants who went astray, searching for food,
Stealing the fruit of myths buried beneath the ground.

At this moment, the details of time have become grains
That I can hold in my hand.
The gold that the archaeologist holds in his palm
Is cold, not because of amnesia,
But because love has been absent for too long.

How pretentious! The two centimeters swept away by the broom
Is actually a new height of the sky.
Are you a Sichuanese? If so, your glory
Has already spanned three thousand years.

I am a Sichuanese, but I am a person buried in sunlight.
Poetry is my relic,
And those ancestors who buried themselves in the soil,
Golden Sands is your relic.

I do not hope for future generations to find me in my ruins,
Just as I do not wish to encounter love,
Soft as gold, in your ruins.

你們留下的不是暗藏玄機的遺言
是金筆碧輝煌的謊言
被現世喧囂喚醒的遺址
一群幽靈訴說的光芒
其實是光陰的血

What you left behind is not a secret will,

But golden, splendid lies.

The ruins awakened by the clamor of the present,

A group of ghosts telling tales of light,

But that light is the blood of time.

二　太陽神鳥

如果不是以金為質　還那麼眩目嗎
我知道你的魂飛去了天堂
但你不是精衛　因為你知道
高度愈高的傳說愈能神秘得讓人膜拜
而祈願　只在民間的低處
太沉　你帶不走

你醒來的時代淌滿流動的金屬
信仰的馬匹吃著幾個世紀以前的草料
營養不良　暗夜如塋
拴養不再柔軟的心跳

沒有翅膀的太陽　會飛
沒有翅膀　是你被埋葬的理由麼
為你虛構翅膀的人
他們　想飛

不是太陽的化身麼
為什麼眷念這終日陰霾的天空
眾生仰望的高處
是一座叫做天堂的墓

出發之前　你給自己鍍上金身
和我們相距兩公分的距離
你其實早已洞悉
人類崇拜的其實是金
不是太陽

II: The Sun God Bird

If not made of gold, would you still be so dazzling?
I know your soul has flown to heaven,
But you are not the mythological bird, because you know,
The higher the legend, the more mysteriously it makes people worship,
And prayers only belong to the low places among the people.
Too heavy, you cannot carry it away.

The time you awoke in was filled with flowing metals,
The horses of faith ate the fodder from centuries ago,
Nutritionally insufficient, the dark night like a tomb,
Tethering the once soft heartbeat.

The sun without wings—does it fly?
Is your burial reasoned in not having wings?
The ones who fabricated wings for you—
They, too, long to fly.

Aren't you the incarnation of the sun?
Why do you cling to this ever-cloudy sky?
The high places that all beings look up to
Are a tomb called Heaven.

Before you left, you coated yourself in gold,
And the two-centimeter distance between us,
You already knew—
What humans worship is actually gold,
Not the sun.

三 面具

在逼近你之前 我先逼退了自己
儘管我是如此平凡的一介俗人
我還是想 能夠戴上這金面具
讓整個世界成為裸體

是的 你需要行走的軀體
而我需要一副行走的面具
我沒有法力附體於你
你也無法借屍還魂

所以 我和你的距離
遠不止三千年
而我和這個世界的距離
只是一副面具

III: The Mask

Before approaching you, I first retreated from myself,
Although I am but an ordinary person,
I still wish to wear this golden mask,
To make the whole world naked.

Yes, you need a body to walk,
And I need a walking mask,
I have no power to possess you,
And you cannot resurrect through my corpse.

So, the distance between you and me,
Is far more than three thousand years.
And the distance between me and the world
Is only a mask.

四 陶罐

你精緻的曲線 獨特的造型
原本出自一雙老繭密佈 粗糙的手
活到今天的不是你泥塑的身胚
是那雙手不死的神奇

做你的是泥土 埋你的是泥土
塑你的是手 刨出你的也是手
可你是手塑形的泥土 且惟一
所以你的身價遠遠高於塑你的手和泥土

但我想把你交給另一雙手
粗糙 更沒有什麼價值
但經過它的裝填
你就不再是徒具的形骸

都說四川鄉村的豆瓣兒很香
農家的酒更香 忘掉身價
你也可以很香

IV: The Pottery

Your exquisite curves, your unique form,
Were originally shaped by a pair of rough, aged hands.
What lives today is not your clay body,
But the immortality of those hands.

Made of earth, buried in earth,
Shaped by hands, dug out by hands,
But you, molded by hands, are one of a kind,
So your value far exceeds the hands and earth that formed you.

But I want to hand you over to another pair of hands,
Rougher, less valuable,
But through their filling,
You will no longer be just a hollow shape.

They say Sichuan village's bean paste is fragrant,
And the country wine smells even better. Forget your value,
You too can be fragrant.

五 象牙

我凝視你的第一秒　只是白的顏色
第二秒　有黑色的聲音浸透脊背
第三秒　一片濺響的血光

我看見　曠古的荒野上
一群大象奔跑　並沒有利刀和槍戟追趕
時光倒退得很快　負重的大地淪陷
森林消失　綠洲消失　沃野消失

洪荒之上　我們的始祖誕生
當征伐成為與肉體無關的本能
被剝落的象牙　你祭祀的
其實是最華麗的原罪

此刻　在我眼中的呈現
是一堆價值昂貴的象牙
更是一種罪證　我轉身
黯然中　你彷彿還原了初時的白

V: Ivory

The first second I gaze at you, you are just the color white,
The second second, black sounds seep through my spine,
The third second, a splash of bloodlight.

I see ancient wilderness,
A group of elephants running, No knives or spears pursuing them,
Time rewinds quickly, the heavy earth collapses,
The forest disappears, the oasis disappears, the fertile land disappears.

Above the primeval chaos, our ancestors were born.
When conquest becomes an instinct unrelated to the body,
The ivory you sacrificed
Is, in fact, the most splendid original sin.

At this moment, the scene before my eyes
Is a pile of expensive ivory,
But more so, it is a piece of evidence. I turn away,
And in the dimness, you seem to revert to your original white.

www.ingramcontent.com/pod-product-compliance
Lightning Source LLC
Chambersburg PA
CBHW060510080526
44586CB00012B/448